DISTRACTING OURSELVES TO DEATH

How to find purpose in a bewildering digital world

REHAN KHAN

DISTRACTING OURSELVES TO DEATH
Copyright © 2021 REHAN KHAN
First published in 2021

Print: 978-1-922456-62-5
E-book: 978-1-922456-63-2
Hardback: 978-1-922456-61-8

All rights reserved. No part of this book may be reproduced, stored in a retrieval system, or transmitted by any means (electronic, mechanical, photocopying, recording, or otherwise) without written permission from the author.

Because of the dynamic nature of the Internet, any web addresses or links contained in this book may have changed since publication and may no longer be valid. The information in this book is based on the author's experiences and opinions. The views expressed in this book are solely those of the author and do not necessarily reflect the views of the publisher; the publisher hereby disclaims any responsibility for them.

The author of this book does not dispense any form of medical, legal, financial, or technical advice either directly or indirectly. The intent of the author is solely to provide information of a general nature to help you in your quest for personal development and growth. In the event you use any of the information in this book, the author and the publisher assume no responsibility for your actions. If any form of expert assistance is required, the services of a competent professional should be sought.

Publishing information
Publishing, design, and production facilitated by Passionpreneur Publishing,
A division of Passionpreneur Organization Pty Ltd, ABN: 48640637529

www.PassionpreneurPublishing.com
Melbourne, VIC | Australia

TABLE OF CONTENTS

TESTIMONIALS	VII

ACT I

1	OUR JOURNEY		5
2	STRUGGLING TO CONCENTRATE		11
	2.1	COGNITIVE COSTS	11
	2.2	HAZARDS OF TASK SWITCHING	14
	2.3	REMEMBERING LESS	16
	2.4	MIND WANDERING	19
	2.5	EXERCISE: APPLYING SINGLE-TASKING	20
	2.6	KEY POINTS	22
3	ALWAYS DISTRACTED		25
	3.1	ATTENTION HACKING	25
	3.2	DOPAMINE PRODUCTION	29
	3.3	MENTAL HEALTH CRISIS	31
	3.4	COLLABORATION IN THE OFFICE	34
	3.5	COGNITIVELY DEMANDING WORK	36
	3.6	EXERCISE: MANAGING YOUR ATTENTION	39
	3.7	EXERCISE: WHAT DO YOU VALUE?	41
	3.8	KEY POINTS	42

ACT II

4 ATTENTION OVERLOAD   49
- 4.1 LIMITED ATTENTION   49
- 4.2 PACKING TOO MUCH   53
- 4.3 UNLOADING THE MIND   55
- 4.4 EXERCISE: IMPACT   58
- 4.5 KEY POINTS   59

5 PRACTICES AND HABITS   63
- 5.1 LEVELS   63
- 5.2 CHARACTER-BASED HABITS   66
- 5.3 IMPROVING HABITS   68
- 5.4 EXERCISE: THREE THINGS TO DO   71
- 5.5 FIVE-MINUTE INSTRUCTION   72
- 5.6 KEY POINTS   74

6 ENVIRONMENTAL TRIGGERS   77
- 6.1 ENVIRONMENT IS KEY   77
- 6.2 FAMILY AND FRIENDS   79
- 6.3 PROXIMITY AND CONFORMITY   81
- 6.4 PRIMING   85
- 6.5 IMPLEMENTATION INTENTION   89
- 6.6 FIRMER INTENTIONS   91
- 6.7 DIDEROT EFFECT   93
- 6.8 EXERCISE: BUILDING HABITS   94
- 6.9 KEY POINTS   96

ACT III

7 MINIMISING DISTRACTION   103
- 7.1 WHAT IS NECESSARY   103
- 7.2 ACHIEVERS IRONY   104

TABLE OF CONTENTS

	7.3	DIGITAL RESTRAINT	107
	7.4	APPLYING IT	109
	7.5	EXERCISE	111
	7.6	KEY POINTS	112
8	OPERATING MODES		115
	8.1	DEALING WITH DISTRACTIONS	115
	8.2	OPERATING AT DEPTH	116
	8.3	OPERATING IN THE SHALLOWS	119
	8.4	EXERCISE: DISCONNECT	126
	8.5	KEY POINTS	127
9	BEING SELECTIVE		129
	9.1	STALLING	129
	9.2	HOW TO SAY "NO"	133
	9.3	RULE OF 9	136
	9.4	PASSION AT WORK IS RARE	138
	9.5	EXERCISE: BECOMING PRESENT	140
	9.6	KEY POINTS	141

ACT IV

10	ATTENTION ENDURANCE		145
	10.1	MAKING YOUR WORK HARDER	145
	10.2	INTELLECT CAN BE CULTIVATED	147
	10.3	PRIME TIME	148
	10.4	RITUALS	149
	10.5	KEY POINTS	153
11	RECHARGING		157
	11.1	SLEEPING FOR THE JOB	157
	11.2	MAINTAINING ENERGY	160
	11.3	REFUEL MIND AND BODY	162
	11.4	KEY POINTS	164

12	**TRANSFORMING**	**167**
12.1	LEARNING A CRAFT	167
12.2	SET BOUNDARIES	173
12.3	INHERENT BELIEFS	175
12.4	DEFIANCE IS POSSIBLE	178
12.5	KEY POINTS	185
13	**EPILOGUE**	**189**
14	**ACKNOWLEDGEMENTS**	**191**
15	**ABOUT THE AUTHOR AND RESOURCES**	**195**

TESTIMONIALS

Rehan has managed to assemble a wonderful and practical guide to being more effective with one's time. He uses just the right mix of evidence coupled with relevance and personal examples, all presented in a fast-paced journey that itself is a case study in micro-learning instructional design. The timing of this book could not be more apropos given all the shifts and pivots that people are experiencing in their work and lives. If you take away and apply only one of the numerous tips presented here, your time was well spent.

**– Brad Boyson, Cofounder, HR Learn In;
Former Executive Director, SHRM Dubai.**

Rehan allows us to pause and reflect on the world around us. Using neuroscience and expert opinion he explores how the forces of distraction can have an adverse impact on our work, our objectives, and our general well-being. Some of the data is quite alarming while at the same time makes complete sense. In this creative storytelling method, we are introduced to a number of themes and concepts which allow us to start thinking more cognitively about how things can affect us. I have collected a number of tips for my tool bag which I will start using in order to maximize my impact both at work and at home.

> – Toneya Sarwar, Human Resources Business Partner, EMEAR, Cisco Systems.

A timely and deeply insightful set of ideas to equip you with the right mindset and practical tools to rein in distraction and increase your personal productivity.

> – Muhammed Mekki, Founding Partner, AstroLabs.

Rehan has deep practitioner experience and real-world industry knowledge. He delivers valuable business insights to clients.

> – Dr. Amanda Nimon-Peters, Business School Professor, Research Fellow, Corporate Speaker.

It is my very pleasure to write these words for my dear colleague Rehan, who has been a trusted thought-partner for me for a few years now. He brings the professionalism, intellectual analytical sharpness, and tenacity of an executive to his work, marrying this with his creative energy and his instincts about personal purpose and meaning. All of that comes with a congenial and expansive, yet focused way of exploring topics and projects whenever we meet or dialogue.

> – Dr. Olaf J. Groth, Global strategist, Think tank founder, Professor, Author, Board member.

TESTIMONIALS

Rehan understands the accelerated pace at which the world of work is changing, and hence it has been a pleasure to tap into his insights for Gulf Business' 'Future' section. Not one to mince his words and always willing to call out the vices of procrastination and distraction in the workplace, he also encourages the positives of flexible working and attaining the elusive work-life balance. I think it's safe to say, this book will be no distraction!

– Aarti Nagraj, Editor, *Gulf Business*.

Rehan is a deeply thoughtful and engaging person. He has a unique ability to see into the human condition and translate his insights into actionable changes. I have made shifts in my life based on Rehan's influence that have made me a more effective and powerful leader.

– Dr. Corrie J. Block, CEO, Paragon Consulting.

Packed with practical advice, built on science, research, and the educator's own personal experiences. I'd highly recommend it for anyone who wants to create more time for the important things in life.

– Wasif Khan, Principal, Corporate Operational Risk.

I'm always impressed with the quality of Rehan's work, the level of thought that goes into each of his deliverables, and the types of insight he gains from working closely with customers. Feedback from each engagement is always positive, with numerous customers requesting him by name for follow-up pieces of work.

– Nathan Kulinitsch, Head of Consulting & Industry Segment Teams (CIST) at Amazon Web Services.

Rehan is a highly experienced and versatile business thought-leader able to articulate to customers how to deliver real business benefits for their particular situation. Customers respect him and colleagues enjoy working with him.

– Chris Bruce, Managing Director, GlobalReach Technology.

I've very much appreciated the opportunity to work with Rehan. Rehan brings a level of thoughtfulness, structure, maturity and insight to any business problem which is a step above the usual standard. He would be my go to person for anything requiring a considered approach to make the complex, simple. It also helps that Rehan is consistently engaging, empathetic, and all round pleasant to work with.

– Max Parry, Senior Director, Business Development, Equinix.

Rehan brings valuable, strategic and relevant insight which differentiates him from others and creates lasting customer relationships.

– Leo Whyte, TMT Consulting, Transformation & Change.

TESTIMONIALS

Rehan is an outstanding thinker who is able to provide solutions and counsel across varied dimensions of business problems and situations. His ability to collaborate and gel in multicultural environments and lead by example is inspiring. I am glad our paths crossed.

– **Mayank Dhingra, Senior Education Business Leader, Middle East, Africa and Eastern Europe, HP.**

Rehan is a highly experienced thought leader. He builds great client relationship and delivers high quality outcomes every time.

– **Imran Hussain, Regional Director, BT, Global Sales Leader, CX Transformation, Customer Success, Delivery.**

Having worked with Rehan over several years, I've always found him to be thoughtful, inspiring and strategic thinker. He is someone with a firm grasp of critical ideas and concepts. He brings a deep understanding to his work and is often mindful of the things others only become aware of much later.

– **Wael El Kabbany, Managing Director Enterprise MEA, Microsoft.**

Rehan is a strong analytical and strategic thinker with an ability to convey his message in a clear, professional and compelling manner at any level in the business.

– **Ian Dench, Chief Executive Officer, Ooredoo Oman.**

*For Irfan, for whom acuity is second nature,
and to whom I am grateful*

ACT I

Chapter 1
OUR JOURNEY

> How astonishing is he who flees from what is inescapable and searches for what is evanescent! "For surely it is not the eyes that are blind, but blind are the hearts which are in the breasts"
>
> – Ibn Ata-illah Al-Iskandari.

Everyone is busy these days. Jumping from one thing to the next. Feeling a real sense of exhilaration. Yet, at the same time, people feel exhausted, overwhelmed, like there's not enough time in the day to get things done.

This isn't an accident. Our digital lives have been designed to keep us distracted, and when we are preoccupied and sidetracked by the trivial, we go through life without purpose or a sense of meaning. In fact, the busier we get, the less we seem to accomplish and the less happy we seem to be. I feel it. You feel it. It's why you have decided to read a book called *Distracting Ourselves to Death*.

As a storyteller, I have divided our journey into four acts. It follows the classic arc of the hero's journey. In this book, you are the protagonist of the story.

- In Act I, we become aware of the level of distraction and why it's happening.
- In Act II, we will react to the problem and step into the unknown.
- In Act III, we actively initiate a response to the problem.
- In Act IV, we step up, confront the issue and undergo a transformation.

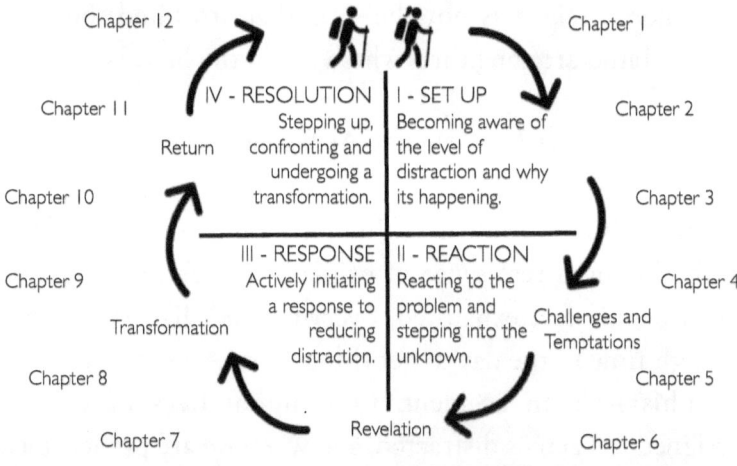

In Act I (Chapters 1, 2, 3), we will understand the true impact of how our digital lives keep us moving from one thing to the next, incessantly preoccupied by the inconsequential, so much so that an entire lifetime can pass by before we truly grasp its purpose and meaning. We will explore what the cognitive costs are of being distracted by something new and novel as well as the effects of multitasking. We will examine why minimising distraction and respecting the attention of users reduces revenues for the attention-economy companies such as Google, Facebook, and the other social-media giants. We will look at how this is creating anxiety amongst the young, the inevitable fallout for organisations, and, of most concern, how we are losing our ability to do cognitively demanding work, which is precisely the skill we need to get ahead in the highly competitive information economy.

Having understood the seriousness of the problem of distraction and why it is happening, we will follow up in Act II (Chapters 4, 5, 6) by examining how our brains are constantly making choices, what chunks of information to process and what to ignore, and how to separate a signal from the noise. We will see what combinations of tasks fit comfortably within our attentional space, and how when our attention is overloaded, we are more likely to make mistakes. We will inspect how when changing our habits, we must also consider the results (the upshot of what we desire), our practices (our methods, routines and procedures), and our character (who we really are). We will observe how practices develop over time, and discover how to instil good habits with a positive trigger, while being mindful of our environment and the role of proximity and conformity. We will survey how even vague intentions boost your odds of successfully carrying out what we intend by 20–30 per cent. However, when we set more specific intentions, the chances rise to 62–91 per cent.

The ground has been set in Act II for how you react to the problem of distraction in your life, so that you are ready in Act III (Chapters 7, 8, 9) to actively initiate a response to dealing with distraction. We will start this act by inspecting how to gain momentum towards what you should be doing by paying attention to what is necessary. It is not about how much you do – it is about doing the right things, the necessary things. The majority of people have not asked themselves what their purpose in life is, what they want to spend their limited time on, and what they should avoid. For example, would it not be prudent to spend our online time on a few carefully chosen activities, which support the things we value? Fortunately, most of the distractions in life can be constrained; this is a hopeful position to start from. When you are doing cognitively demanding work and you remove distractions, you can maintain your energy levels for much longer. We will learn how to overcome procrastination, which we all fall victim to, and how to say no with sophistication and delicacy, and to only take on tasks when utterly convinced of their benefit. Our discussion will explore why you need to approach work like a craftsman, and how this will lead you to become passionate about it.

The response you initiate in Act III will then set up the transformation required in your life, and this will be explored further in Act IV (Chapters 10, 11, 12). One way to reduce the amount of time we aimlessly let our minds wander is to deliberately make our tasks harder. When we cognitively stretch our minds and our tasks are complex enough to consume our attentional space, we have greater scope to grow our intelligence. We will examine the importance of maintaining energy levels, as well as how a lack of sleep can fundamentally hinder your ability to perform at your peak and leads to other damaging physical and emotional side effects. Finally, we will study how when we immerse ourselves in a craft, and leave the digital world, it makes us more human, and we obtain deeper satisfaction from life itself. We will discuss how to renovate your life with meaningful pursuits so you avoid digital distractions, and the importance of setting boundaries in your life so that you don't become spread too thin. We will end this section by looking at how human qualities, such as intellectual skills, can be cultivated, and how to defy the attention merchants trying to distract you away from your true purpose in life.

There will be a lot for you to consider as you go through the material. Take your time. I want you to understand the magnitude of the problem before you try to find a way out. I can be your guide and show you the way. But, remember, you are the protagonist and the hero of your own journey away from a life of distraction and towards one of purpose.

At times, some of what you read will be uncomfortable, as the truth of how much time we spend on trivia becomes apparent. In fact, you will be wrenched out of your comfort zone. But in the long run, it will be worth facing this inconvenient reality, as you will get your life back and become more productive and fulfilled as a person in your work and your personal life.

Chapter 2
STRUGGLING TO CONCENTRATE

> The unexamined life is not worth living
>
> – Socrates.

2.1 Cognitive costs

Every person seems to be busy these days. Ask anyone how they are doing and the standard response is "I'm busy" and, generally, their busyness involves their smartphones: people are walking along whilst sending a message, standing in a queue whilst browsing their phone, or sitting with a real friend whilst chatting with other friends online. In other words, we seem to be doing an incredible amount of multi-tasking, at all times.

But how much are we actually accomplishing?

According to Earl Miller, a neuroscientist at MIT and one of the world's experts on divided attention, our brains are "not wired to multitask well ... When people think they're multitasking, they're actually just switching from one task to another very rapidly, and every time they do, there's a cognitive cost in doing so."[1] Though not visible immediately, the cognitive cost is quite tangible and consists of the following:

- Multitasking increases production of the stress hormone cortisol as well as the fight-or-flight hormone adrenaline, which can overstimulate the brain, initiating dazed or misty thoughts to take hold of us. When we read the biographies of former senior executives or people high-up in government, they say often the worst decisions they made were when they had too many things going on at the same time. In that moment, they just lost all sense of clarity and a kind of haze set in.
- What is also going on is that the prefrontal cortex, the part of the brain we rely on for staying on task and helping us focus, becomes easily hijacked by anything new or novel. Responding to a notification, scrolling through social-media sites, checking email – each of these new or novel things fires off the neurochemical dopamine. Dopamine makes us feel good. It's akin to sweets for the brain – we receive a rush of dopamine as we switch tasks.

With dopamine firing off as we toggle between tasks, we feel great. In other words, multitasking provides us with a feeling of enjoyment – it's fun. Yet, we get less done. If you are serious about addressing distraction in your life so that you become more fulfilled and productive in the things that matter, then the true measure is not how busy you are, but what you accomplish.

Stanford researchers Eyal Ophir, Clifford Nass, and Anthony Wagner undertook a multitasking study to determine what made, as the conventional wisdom seemed to suggest, heavy multitaskers more effective.[2]

- First, they tested whether multitaskers were better at ignoring irrelevant information. They were not. The heavy multitaskers' "performance was horrible".
- When that failed, the researchers tested whether multitaskers were better at storing and organising information or had better memories. They were not, and didn't.
- Stumped, they conducted a third test to see if multitaskers were better at switching between tasks. They were not, and, to make things worse, the light multitaskers in the study were better at multitasking than the heavy multitaskers! "They couldn't help thinking about the task they weren't doing," Ophir said. "They can't keep things separate in their minds."

As Ophir put it: "We kept looking for what they're better at, and we didn't find it." The multitaskers perceived that they performed better because their brains were more stimulated, but in every single study, they performed worse.

Multitaskers are not only accomplishing less, they are also compounding their stress levels by flooding their brains with cortisol and adrenalin.

2.2 Hazards of task switching

In work led by Gloria Mark, a professor of information science at the University of California and one of the world's foremost experts on attention and multitasking, a team conducted attentional studies in partnership with NASA, Boeing, Intel, IBM, and Microsoft.

With users' permission, Mark and her team installed a logging program on participants' computers to observe exactly how often they switched between tasks. Astonishingly, it was very forty seconds. Now, remember, according to Professor Earl Miller, when you switch tasks, there is a cognitive cost – cortisol and adrenaline get fired off. The result is we are often left exhausted, feeling like there are not enough hours in the day, and that we are always behind the eight ball.

The research also revealed that when users were deep in a flow state, concentrating on a task with their full attention, and were then distracted – perhaps by a colleague in an open-plan office approaching them, or when the lure of their smartphone was too much – in others words, they picked up their device and disappeared into a digital black hole for some time. When they went back to the original task they

STRUGGLING TO CONCENTRATE

were concentrating on, it would, on average, take 25 minutes to return to the same level of cognitive depth they were at before being interrupted.

What makes matters worse is that we do not actually go back to the original task straight away, but, on average, we end up doing 2.26 other tasks before going back to the initial one.

In adjacent research performed by Mark and her colleagues into the cost and impact of constant interruptions, the findings were quite revealing:

> When people are constantly interrupted, they develop a mode of working faster (and writing less) to compensate for the time they know they will lose by being interrupted. Yet working faster with interruptions has its cost: people in the interrupted conditions experienced a higher workload, more stress, higher frustration, more time pressure, and effort. So interrupted work may be done faster, but at a price ...
>
> Our results suggest that interruptions lead people to change not only work rhythms but also strategies and mental states. Another possibility is that interruptions do in fact lengthen the time to perform a task but that this extra time only occurs directly after the interruption when reorienting back to the task, and it can be compensated for by a faster and more stressful working style.[3]

Now think about this. You are trying to get something done. It needs your full attention and the whole day can go by and you do not accomplish it. We have all been there. In order to mitigate this, we try to work faster, but this frenetic state creates unwanted stress, and can lead to lower quality deliverables being produced, further compounding mental strain and physical fatigue.

2.3 Remembering less

Constant interruptions – whether they are from people or are electronic – create stress. Glenn Wilson, a former visiting professor of psychology at King's College, London University, found that being in a situation where you are trying to concentrate on a task and an email is sitting unread in your inbox can reduce your effective IQ by 10 points.[4]

The research with 1,100 people showed high levels of doziness, lethargy and an inability to focus when people are constantly interrupted, with emails in particular having an addictive, drug-like grip on respondents. Those in the research group found themselves all over the place every time an email appeared in their inbox. Productivity took a hit as employees could not resist the temptation to dip into messages, taking them away from their actual work. "This is a very real and widespread phenomenon," said Wilson.

The most damage occurred as a result of respondents' complete lack of discipline in how they fielded emails. There was a compulsion to reply to each new message immediately, which distracted the brain and slowed it down when performing other tasks. Wilson advised that: "Companies should encourage a more balanced and appropriate way of working."

According to Wilson, the loss of 10 IQ points is more than the cognitive loss from smoking marijuana, which reduces effective IQ by about six points. As a side note, the reason marijuana impacts IQ is that it activates dedicated cannabinol receptors in the brain and interferes with memory and our ability to concentrate on several things at once.

Elsewhere, Stanford neuroscientist Russ Poldrack found that learning information while multitasking causes the new information to go to the wrong part of the brain.[5] If students study and watch TV at the same time, the information from their studies goes into the striatum, a region dedicated to storing new procedures and skills, such as learning how to juggle, not facts and ideas. Without TV distracting the students, the information enters the hippocampus, where it is structured and classified in a variety of ways, making recall easier later on. Poldrack explained:

> When we learn while we multitask, we rely more heavily on the basal ganglia, a brain system that's involved in the learning of skills and habits. [However] when we encode information in a more focussed state, we rely more heavily on our brain's hippocampus – which actually lets us store and recall the information.

The same holds true when we undergo professional training and learn new information whilst simultaneously surfing our smartphones – the information ends up in the striatum, which stores new procedures and skills as opposed to facts and ideas. If we had been paying full attention, the information would have been encoded in the hippocampus, where it is arranged and classified, making it simpler for our brain to recover later.

There are also the metabolic costs I mentioned earlier, which are summarised by Daniel Levitin author of *The Organized Mind* (2015):

> Asking the brain to shift attention from one activity to another causes the prefrontal cortex and striatum to burn up oxygenated glucose, the same fuel they need to stay on task. And the kind of rapid, continual shifting we do with multitasking causes the brain to burn through fuel so quickly that we feel exhausted and disoriented after even a short time. We've literally depleted the nutrients in our brain. This leads to compromises in both cognitive and physical performance.
>
> Among other things, repeated task switching leads to anxiety, which raises levels of the stress hormone cortisol in the brain, which in turn can lead to aggressive and impulsive behaviour. By contrast, staying on task is controlled by the anterior cingulate and the striatum, and once we engage the central executive mode, staying in that state uses less energy than multitasking and actually reduces the brain's need for glucose.[6]

2.4 Mind wandering

As we take a cognitive hit, primarily from stress, due to interruptions and end up cataloguing information in the wrong part of the brain due to distractions, what also happens is that we think a lot about what we are not doing presently. We are either pondering over the past, reflecting on what might happen in the future, or musing about what could have happened but did not. As described by psychologists Matthew A. Killingsworth and Daniel T. Gilbert of Harvard University in the journal *Science*: "A human mind is a wandering mind, and a wandering mind is an unhappy mind." Killingsworth and Gilbert write: "The ability to think about what is not happening is a cognitive achievement that comes at an emotional cost."[7]

The psychologists developed an iPhone app that contacted 2,250 volunteers at random intervals to ask how happy they were, what they were currently doing, and whether they were thinking about their current activity or about something else that was pleasant, neutral, or unpleasant. The respondents selected from 22 general activities, such as eating, shopping, walking, and watching television. Remarkably, subjects reported that 46.9 per cent of the time, their minds were wandering. In other words, they were not present in whatever they were doing, whether that was eating a meal with the family, talking with friends, or doing a work task.

"Mind wandering appears ubiquitous across all activities," says Killingsworth. "This study shows that our mental lives are pervaded, to a remarkable degree, by the non-present."

The researchers believe the mind wandering is an excellent predictor of people's happiness. Time-lag analyses suggested that their respondents' mind wandering was generally the cause, not the consequence, of their unhappiness.

"Many philosophical and religious traditions teach that happiness is to be found by living in the moment, and practitioners are trained to resist mind wandering and to 'be here now'," Killingsworth and Gilbert note in *Science*. "These traditions suggest that a wandering mind is an unhappy mind."

Being present and single-tasking, as opposed to mind wandering and multitasking, is one of the best ways to concentrate on fulfilling the need of the moment and come away from it feeling content and happy.

2.5 Exercise: Applying single-tasking

The only way we are going to make the change from multitasking to single-tasking is if we apply these principles to the situations in which we find ourselves. For a start, try the following:

- Paying attention during virtual meetings: It is really easy to start letting your attention drift when you are on a conference call, particularly if it is audio-only. We itch to check emails, messages and social-media notifications. Every time this happens, really focus hard on directing your attention back to the call. This very act will strengthen your ability to focus, as you will be using exercising your attention muscle. If you keep relapsing, perhaps due to the content on the call, ask yourself whether you actually need to be on the call or not, and whether it would be better to be doing something else related to your work at this time.

- Actively listening: There are times when we sit with someone but we do not take in much of what they are saying. We might be nodding in agreement but we are not genuinely listening. When you actively listen to someone, you bring all your attention to the conversation you are having. You do not think about a clever response to what they are saying, but you just consider their words and allow yourself time to reflect on them. People genuinely appreciate it when you bring complete attention to the conversation. One of the things I sometimes do when I meet someone, particularly a new person, is that I switch my smartphone into airplane mode so I create the right conditions to focus just on the conversation in front of me. People genuinely appreciate this type of behaviour.
- Reading with flow: Unfortunately, fewer and fewer knowledge workers and professionals are actually spending time reading, either fiction or non-fiction, preferring instead to use their devices to receive bite-size content, which encourages swiping through

information and skimming from one headline to the next, but never truly penetrating the subject matter in a long read. As a novelist, I would obviously encourage you to read for the sheer thrill and exhilaration you will obtain by losing yourself completely in a gripping novel, but even if you address the matter purely from the perspective of productivity, when you are deep in a book, you are strengthening your attention muscle, your ability to stay focused. This is a vital skill in the professional world and will continue to become more important as the level of distraction escalates around us.

2.6 Key points

Some of the critical points we covered in this chapter were as follows:

- Our digital lives have been designed to keep us distracted, and when we are preoccupied and sidetracked by the trivial, we go through life without purpose or a sense of meaning.
- Every time you switch from one task to another very rapidly, there's a cognitive cost to doing so.
- Multitaskers are not only accomplishing less, they are also compounding their stress levels by flooding their brains with cortisol and adrenalin.

- Every time you are distracted when deeply concentrating on a task, on average, it takes 25 minutes to return to the same level of cognitive depth you were at before being interrupted, and often you will do 2.26 other tasks before going back to the initial one.
- When you are trying to concentrate on a task, and an email is sitting unread in your inbox, it can reduce your effective IQ by 10 points.
- Learning information while multitasking causes the new information to go to the wrong part of the brain.
- Our minds wander 47 per cent of the time. In other words, we are not present in whatever we are doing. Additionally, a wandering mind has been shown to be an unhappy mind.

Endnotes

1. Daniel J. Levitin, *The Organized Mind: Thinking Straight in the Age of Information Overload*, 2015.
2. Stanford, "Media multitaskers pay mental price", https://news.stanford.edu/2009/08/24/multitask-research-study-082409/.
3. Gloria Mark, *"The Cost of Interrupted Work: More Speed and Stress"*, University of California.
4. "Emails pose threat to IQ", *The Guardian*, 22 April 2005.
5. Karin Foerde, Barbara J. Knowlton, and Russell A. Poldrack, "Modulation of competing memory systems by distraction", *Proceedings of the National Academy of Science USA*, 103(31), 1 August 2006, pp. 11778-11783.
6. Daniel J. Levitin, *The Organized Mind: Thinking Straight in the Age of Information Overload*, 2015.
7. Matthew A. Killingsworth and Daniel T. Gilbert, "A Wandering Mind Is an Unhappy Mind", *Science*, Vol. 330, Issue 6006, 12 Nov 2010, pp. 932.

Chapter 3
ALWAYS DISTRACTED

> Our greatest glory is not in never falling, but in rising every time we fall
>
> – Confucius.

3.1 Attention hacking

As we observed in the previous chapter, we are struggling to concentrate. We keep switching tasks even though it is hazardous to our health, and when we learn in a distracted state, the information ends up going into the wrong part of the brain, where we can't access and retrieve it later on. How did we, as humanity, collectively get ourselves into this situation?

I started working in the telecoms and technology sector back in 1993, and I certainly didn't sign up for this type of future, where my working and private time would be shattered

DISTRACTING OURSELVES TO DEATH

into a thousand shards by incessant digital distractions. Did you? Probably not, but this present-day distraction crisis we are in is no accident. Here is why.

When the late Steve Jobs launched the first Apple iPhone in 2007, I, like millions of others, purchased it with great excitement and awe. We were on our way to a general-purpose mobile computer, the like of which we had seen the crew of *Star Trek* using. Paid Wi-Fi was being actively rolled out in many public locations, enabling emails to be accessed from any location, but back then, there was no app store, no social-media notifications, nor services like Instagram.

In fact, if you watch Jobs' keynote address when launching the original iPhone, what do you think the killer app was? It will probably come as a complete surprise to you, but according to Jobs, the killer app was "making calls".[1]

Now, remember back then we used to have a phone from a company like Nokia, Ericsson, or Motorola, and there were those who had a Blackberry and were addicted to them. Then, people also walked around with an iPod, for listening to music. The result was we had two devices in our pockets. Now, along comes the iPhone, which enabled your iPod to make calls. That was the "killer app". In the keynote, it's not until 33 minutes into the presentation that Jobs gets around to highlighting features like improved text messaging and mobile internet access.

I think if you had told me in 2007 that in the near future the average iPhone user would obsessively check their device 80 times a day,[2] I would have been the first one to abandon it. Nowadays, Apple even has an app on the phone called Screen Time to show how often you are using the phone. They know how addictive it is.

I am not really sure this is the type of digital world we wanted, but it is the one we got. Sometimes, you arrive at a place that is not where you want to be, but at a place where you need to be. Maybe this is one of those moments – when upon seeing this great force of distraction and antagonism rearing itself up, we can finally wake up, and do something about it.

The obvious follow-up question is: did we arrive in this digital miasma by accident or by design? Unfortunately, many of the digital tools and platforms that tech companies have us hooked on are not as innocent as they appear. Equally, people are not addicted to their screens because human nature is inherently idle or sluggish. The primary reason we are in the present digital disarray is that a handful of technology investors have funnelled billions of dollars into making this a reality.

In a groundbreaking *60 Minutes* segment titled "Brain Hacking", Anderson Cooper interviews Tristan Harris, a former start-up founder and Google engineer who left the comfortable path he was on to become a whistleblower. I would urge you to watch the clip, at least the first six minutes, as it is tremendously revealing.[3]

In the interview, the whistleblower, Harris, says, "This thing is a slot machine," as he holds up his smartphone.

"How is that a slot machine?" Cooper, the interviewer, asks.

"Well, every time I check my phone, I'm playing the slot machine to see 'what did I get?'" Harris answers. "There's a whole playbook of techniques that get used [by technology companies] to get you using the product for as long as possible."

Harris continues, "They are programming people. There's always this narrative that technology's neutral. And it's up to us to choose how we use it. This is just not true—"

"Technology is not neutral?" Cooper interrupts.

Harris responds: "It's not neutral. They want you to use it in particular ways and for long periods of time. Because that's how they make their money."

The reality is that minimising distraction and respecting users' attention reduces revenues. Obsessive use sells, which Harris says drives the attention-economy companies like Google, Facebook, and the other social-media giants. He poignantly calls it "race to the bottom of the brain stem".

In the autumn of 2017, Sean Parker, the founding president of Facebook, spoke openly at an event about the attention engineering deployed by his former company:

> The thought process that went into building these applications, Facebook being the first of them to really understand it, that thought process was all about how do we consume as much of your time and conscious attention as possible?
>
> And that means that we need to sort of give you a little dopamine hit every once in a while, because

someone liked or commented on a photo or post of whatever.[4]

The manner in which our digital lives operate today has been crafted and engineered in boardrooms to serve the interests of a select group of technology investors. It's about time all of us seriously reflect on how we break this addiction, as this is not the digital future we deserve for ourselves, our families and the coming generations, nor should we be cajoled into believing there is nothing we can do about it.

3.2 Dopamine production

I have mentioned the neurochemical dopamine a couple of times, and it was referred to by Sean Parker, the founding President of Facebook. What is it? Dopamine was discovered during an experiment by McGill neuroscientists Peter Milner and James Olds.[5] They placed electrodes in the brains of rats, in a small structure of the limbic system (called the nucleus accumbens). The researchers discovered that this structure within the brain regulates dopamine production.

Olds and Milner called it the pleasure centre. A lever in the cage allowed the rats to send a small electrical signal directly into this part of the limbic system. The rats liked it so much that they did nothing else. They forgot all about eating and sleeping. Long after they were hungry, they ignored tasty food. The rats just pressed the lever over and over again until they died of starvation and exhaustion.

You may be thinking that these were rats and not people. Humans are not so different when it comes to how we are stimulated and the effects of dopamine. According to Dr Natasha Dow Schüll, who has done some really interesting research on gambling habits in Las Vegas, the average slot-machine player will spin the wheel 600 times per hour and be totally fixated with the game they have immersed themselves in.[6] Some will even wear adult pants so they don't need to take a comfort break. She says the same design principles[7] used in slot machines are used for smartphone apps and games like Candy Crush and Angry Birds.[8]

The habits of gamblers can be extreme, but surely a person wouldn't kill themselves in the pursuit of receiving a dopamine hit? Humans have more intelligence than rats that are stimulated to keep pulling a lever. Surely? Unfortunately, a thirty-year-old man died in Beijing, China, after playing video games continuously for three days.[9] Another man died in Taiwan after a three-day video game binge.[10] Others have died in similar circumstances in Guangzhou, China, and Daegu, South Korea, as well as other locations.

People, like the rats in the McGill experiments, are starting to die from the effects of seeking a dopamine fix. Each time we check a Twitter feed or Facebook update, or encounter something new, we get "reward hormones". Yet, it is the novelty-seeking portion of the brain propelling the limbic system that provokes this feeling of pleasure, not the higher-level thought centres in the prefrontal cortex.

Is this really how we should be occupying our lives?

3.3 Mental health crisis

If you and I are struggling with the level of distraction created by technology, then give a thought to iGen. This is the term coined by Professor Jean Twenge, one of the world's foremost experts on generational differences in American youth. iGen are young people born between 1995 and 2012, and they are noticeably different from Millennials.

According to research carried out by Common Sense Media, teenagers in the US were consuming media – including text messaging and social networks – nine hours per day on average.[11] In her *Atlantic* article, entitled "Have Smartphones Destroyed a Generation", Twenge argues that we should be extremely concerned about the psychological health of iGen. She says:

> Psychologically, however, they are more vulnerable than Millennials were: Rates of teen depression and suicide have skyrocketed since 2011. It's not an exaggeration to describe iGen as being on the brink of the worst mental-health crisis in decades. Much of this deterioration can be traced to their phones.
>
> Even when a seismic event—a war, a technological leap, a free concert in the mud—plays an outsize role in shaping a group of young people, no single factor ever defines a generation. Parenting styles continue to change, as do school curricula and culture, and these things matter. But the twin rise

of the smartphone and social media has caused an earthquake of a magnitude we've not seen in a very long time, if ever. There is compelling evidence that the devices we've placed in young people's hands are having profound effects on their lives—and making them seriously unhappy.[12]

According to Twenge, the tectonic shift in mental health coincided exactly with the moment when American smartphone ownership became common. iGen, she explains, grew up with iPhones and social media, and don't remember a time before constant access to the internet.

Twenge continues in her *Atlantic* article:

> What's the connection between smartphones and the apparent psychological distress this generation is experiencing? For all their power to link kids day and night, social media also exacerbate the age-old teen concern about being left out. Today's teens may go to fewer parties and spend less time together in person, but when they do congregate, they document their hangouts relentlessly—on Snapchat, Instagram, Facebook. Those not invited to come along are keenly aware of it. Accordingly, the number of teens who feel left out has reached all-time highs across age groups. Like the increase in loneliness, the upswing in feeling left out has been swift and significant.

This trend has been especially steep among girls. Forty-eight percent more girls said they often felt left out in 2015 than in 2010, compared with 27 percent more boys. Girls use social media more often, giving them additional opportunities to feel excluded and lonely when they see their friends or classmates getting together without them. Social media levy a psychic tax on the teen doing the posting as well, as she anxiously awaits the affirmation of comments and likes.

"The use of social media and smartphones look culpable for the increase in teen mental-health issues," Twenge told journalist Benoit Denizet-Lewis for a feature in *New York Times* magazine.[13] "It's enough for an arrest – and as we get more data, it might be enough for a conviction."

What we are witnessing before us is an entire generation whose behaviour is being changed. Rather than taking time out to just be, to think, to ponder, to reflect, to make sense of the world and build lasting relationships, iGen are, like the rats in the McGill experiment, being underhandedly overstimulated. Their brains are not being given downtime, when they are disconnected from stimuli. This is particularly onerous for them as it coincides with a point in their lives when their minds and body are still undergoing tremendous biological change. They are not being given time to mature into rounded, mature adults but, rather, are being "experimented" on, in the interests of a business model that relies on distraction to make money.

3.4 Collaboration in the office

The very same social media and collaboration platforms that have driven the increase in mental health issues amongst iGen are unfortunately also being rolled out within corporates and organisations around the world. In a world in which workers trade knowledge as their capital – whether that's medical professionals, lawyers, programmers, management consultants, or the majority of other white-collar professions – collaboration, we are told, is king. The ability to work with others who have ideas and knowledge towards a common business goal is the panacea of many a pep-talk from the "C" level. Collaboration, it is narrated, improves efficiency and germinates new ideas. I would concur with this, since, just as no person is an island, no idea forms in a vacuum.

Yet, too often technology evangelists ride into town with their collaboration platforms such as Facebook Workplace, Slack, or a host of others in the market. We are told this is to improve employee collaboration, drive up productivity and foster creativity. In fact, many of these solutions are being introduced into corporations today with the headline "bringing consumer technology experiences into business". This is, in some quarters, being heralded as a major breakthrough in making things easier for employees. Though I am all for making life simpler – who wouldn't be? – I am also really anxious at the lack of consideration organisations are giving to the question of how this is going to impact their employees' mindset and mental health in the long-term.

There are dozens of studies out there citing how social-media platforms like Facebook can be damaging to your mental health.[14] There is even a study from Facebook itself saying that spending time on social media can be bad for you.[15] These platforms prey on anxieties like Fear of Missing Out (FOMO), which is a fear that influences iGen's experience of social media and collaboration platforms.

With these consumer platforms now invading corporate workspaces, there is reason to believe these same anxieties, like FOMO, will snowball amongst workers. We already see this in how some colleagues like to copy everyone in to an email reply, when they have nothing to say but just want to be seen to have said something. This type of behaviour is classic FOMO and only worsened during the global pandemic of 2020, as more workers found themselves working remotely and increasingly feeling lonely and anxious. The situation will only get worse when you weaponise that voice through a company-wide collaboration platform.

But what really makes me nervous is that the generation we call iGen will, within a decade, be entering the workplace and potentially carrying with them all of these built-up mental health issues related to smartphone usage and also exacerbated by the 2020 global pandemic and the forced isolation it brought about. They will also encounter the same consumer-type social and collaboration platforms that have triggered so much anxiety within them in the first place. What is going to be the impact on human resources departments within companies, who today are more used to dealing with compensation and benefits? Will they end up hiring more counsellors and mental health professionals to cope with the rising level of workplace anxiety as a result of overuse of technology? I don't know, but it's worth considering and even planning for in advance.

3.5 Cognitively demanding work

With our attention being hacked, dopamine being fired off, iGen being bombarded by engineered distraction, and workers in organisations facing the same deluge, what concerns me, and should deeply concern you, is that we are losing our ability to do what Professor Cal Newport of Georgetown University calls "deep work". He says that deep work is:

> Professional activities performed in a state of distraction-free concentration that push your cognitive capabilities to their limit. These efforts create new value, improve your skill, and are hard to replicate ...
>
> We now know from decades of research in both psychology and neuroscience that the state of mental strain that accompanies deep work is also necessary to improve your abilities. Deep work, in other words, [is] exactly the type of effort needed to stand out in a cognitively demanding field.[16]

According to Cal Newport, the reason knowledge workers are losing their ability to do deep work is due to distractions from electronic tools – email and SMS, social media networks like Twitter and Facebook, and infotainment sites like BuzzFeed and Reddit. The rise of these tools, combined with access through smartphones and networked office computers, has fragmented most knowledge workers' attention into slivers.

A McKinsey study found that the average knowledge worker now spends more than 60 per cent of the work week engaged in electronic communication and internet searching, with close to 30 per cent of a worker's time dedicated to reading and answering emails alone.[17] This level of distraction is not conducive to prolonged periods of cognitively demanding work.

However, if you walk into most offices, workers seem to be as busy as ever, so what is going on? Well, they are, instead, engaged in what Cal Newport calls "shallow work". He explains shallow work as:

> Non-cognitively demanding, logistical-style tasks, often performed while distracted. These efforts tend not to create much new value in the world and are easy to replicate.
>
> In an age of network tools, in other words, knowledge workers increasingly replace deep work with the shallow alternative—constantly sending and receiving e-mail messages like human network routers, with frequent breaks for quick hits of distraction. Larger efforts that would be well served by deep thinking, such as forming a new business strategy or writing an important grant application, get fragmented into distracted dashes that produce muted quality. To make

matters worse for depth, there's increasing evidence that this shift toward the shallow is not a choice that can be easily reversed. Spend enough time in a state of frenetic shallowness and you permanently reduce your capacity to perform deep work.

The importance and need for knowledge workers to undertake cognitively demanding deep work will only continue to rise. During the Industrial Age, when the majority of workers were targeted with producing parts of a whole, there was not much scope to do deep work, unless you were in the minority who were the skilled and professional class, responsible for running the industrial environment. Much of the world has shifted, rightly or wrongly, to an information economy, in which the majority of those engaged in the labour market are classified as knowledge workers – in this economy, the ability to perform deep work is a sought-after currency.

As a result, anyone who wants to get ahead in the highly competitive global information economy must possess the skills and ability to go deep in their working lives. Those who will be rewarded will not be the ones who consume services, but those who produce them. Unfortunately, fewer and fewer knowledge workers are undertaking deep work, at precisely the moment when it is becoming a highly desired skill within the information economy. As a result, those who can cultivate the skill will be able to set their own terms of how and when they work.

3.6 Exercise: Managing your attention

When you manage your attention deliberately, you choose one important object of attention, eliminating all other distractions. When you concentrate deeply, you become completely immersed in your work. Choosing which tasks to work on ahead of time lets you focus on what's actually important in the moment. This is so crucial in today's knowledge work environments, where not all tasks we are given are of equal importance.

As we begin to focus, as Chris Bailey, author of *Hyperfocus* says, only one meaningful task must be occupying our attentional space. The most critical tasks benefit from every bit of extra attention. They are usually not habits, which by default do not often consume our full attentional space.

As Bailey records, we pass through four states as we begin to focus:

> First, we're focused (and productive). Then, assuming we don't get distracted or interrupted, our mind begins to wander. Third, we make note of this mind wandering. This can take a while, especially if we don't frequently check what is consuming our attentional space. (On average, we notice about five times an hour that our mind has wandered.) And fourth, we shift our focus back to our original object of attention.[18]

Try the following exercise to manage your attention:

1. Choose a meaningful task: Set an intention for what you want to focus on and for how long. If possible, think about where you want to do this. The task you might want to bring your attention to could be writing an important board paper, coaching a colleague, or running a focus group. It doesn't have to be something you undertake in isolation. It's all about your focus and being present in whatever you are doing.
2. Eradicate outer and inner distractions: We often become distracted from what we really should be doing. This is true both at work and at home. Notifications become even more enticing to deal with than the task we should be doing. Remember the study by Glenn Wilson, who said that our effective IQ drops by 10 points when the email notification is highlighted and our attention is drawn to it. The good news is that distractions can be simply dealt with in advance – turn off your notifications and put your phone on flight mode. If its inner thoughts, such as "I need to book my summer holiday this weekend before the prices go up" or "I need to tidy up the living room before we have guests over on Friday night", then keep a separate piece of paper close to hand, and every time a stray thought pops into your head, simply write it down and carry on focusing on the task at hand.

3. Focus on the chosen object of attention: Now, having set your intention and eliminated distractions, focus on the chosen object of attention for a set duration of time.
4. Draw your mind back to the task: Your mind will wander. As research undertaken by psychologists Matthew A. Killingsworth and Daniel T. Gilbert of Harvard University showed, our mind wanders for 47 per cent of the day. If we are awake for 16 hours in a typical day, that means we are not actually present for eight hours. Mind wandering seems to be a default setting for human beings, but if you can train your mind to focus on what is actually going on at this moment, then you can radically improve your effectiveness, productivity and overall satisfaction with your own life.

3.7 Exercise: What do you value?

One of the reasons you may want to eliminate distraction from your life is so that you can spend more time on the things you actually value. The irony here is that too often many of us have never stopped to consider what it really is that we value in life. If that sounds like you, then I would like you to undertake the following activity:

- If you find that you have removed distractions from your life and you now have one hour extra every day, what will you spend this newfound time on?

- To help you answer this, consider the following:
  - What do you really value in life?
  - Why do you want to remove distractions?
  - What do you care most about? This could be related to matters such as learning, family, community, religion, or self-development.
- If you find yourself struggling with the above, then picture for a moment the end of your life. I know it doesn't sound very pleasant, but imagine you are on your deathbed. What would you have a regret about not doing in life? Pondering this existential moment, which we are all heading towards, will definitely help sharpen your mind and crystallise what you value the most.

3.8 Key points

Some of the critical points we covered in this chapter were as follows:

- Our digital lives, with a multitude of distractions, have been designed for the benefit of a handful of technology investors.
- Minimising distraction and respecting users' attention reduces revenues for the attention-economy companies like Google, Facebook, and the other social-media giants.

- Each time we check a Twitter feed or Facebook update, or encounter something new, we get "reward hormones" or a dopamine hit.
- According to research, the tectonic shift in mental health amongst iGen coincides exactly with the moment smartphone ownership became common amongst this generation.
- Social-media platforms prey on anxieties like Fear of Missing Out (FOMO), and these types of platforms are now invading corporate workspaces. As a result, there is reason to believe these same anxieties, like FOMO, will snowball amongst workers.
- With our attention being hacked, dopamine being fired off, iGen being bombarded by engineered distraction, and workers in organisations facing the same deluge, we are losing our ability to do cognitively demanding work.
- Anyone who wants to get ahead in the highly competitive global information economy must possess the skills and quality to go deep in their working lives.

Endnotes

1. Steve Jobs, iPhone 2007 Presentation (HD). YouTube 51:18 recorded 09/01/2007.
2. https://nypost.com/2017/11/08/americans-check-their-phones-80-times-a-day-study/.
3. Tristan Harris interview with Anderson Cooper, *60 Minutes*, https://www.youtube.com/watch?v=awAMTQZmvPE.
4. Sean Parker interview https://www.youtube.com/watch?v=R7jar4KgKxs.
5. J. L. Olds and P. M. Milner, "Positive reinforcement produced by electrical stimulation of septal area and other regions of rat brain," *Journal of Comparative & Physiological Psychology*, 47, 1954, pp. 419–427.
6. Natasha Dow Schüll, *Addiction by Design: Machine Gambling in Las Vegas*, Princeton, NJ, Princeton University Press, 2014.
7. Dr Natasha Dow Schull, lecture at University of Richmond, https://www.youtube.com/watch?v=TazssD6L7wc.
8. Dr Natasha Dow Schull, interview, https://www.youtube.com/watch?v=ETB0x2UU6JE.
9. "Chinese online gamer dies after three-day session", BBC, https://www.bbc.com/news/world-asia-pacific-12541769.
10. "Man dies in Taiwan after 3-day online gaming binge", CNN, https://edition.cnn.com/2015/01/19/world/taiwan-gamer-death/index.html.

11 Common Sense Media, https://www.commonsensemedia.org/about-us/news/press-releases/landmark-report-us-teens-use-an-average-of-nine-hours-of-media-per-day.
12 "Have Smartphones Destroyed a Generation", *The Atlantic*, https://www.theatlantic.com/magazine/archive/2017/09/has-the-smartphone-destroyed-a-generation/534198/.
13 "Why Are More American Teenagers Than Ever Suffering From Severe Anxiety?" *New York Times Magazine*, https://www.nytimes.com/2017/10/11/magazine/why-are-more-american-teenagers-than-ever-suffering-from-severe-anxiety.html.
14 Dr Bridget Dibb, "Social media use and perceptions of physical health", University of Surrey; or Wonseok (Eric) Jang, Erik P. Bucy and Janice Cho, "Self-esteem moderates the influence of self-presentation style on Facebook users' sense of subjective well-being", *Science Direct*.
15 https://about.fb.com/news/2017/12/hard-questions-is-spending-time-on-social-media-bad-for-us/.
16 Cal Newport, *Deep Work*, 2016.
17 "The social economy: Unlocking value and productivity through social technologies", *McKinsey*, 2012.
18 Chris Bailey, *Hyperfocus*, 2018.

ACT II

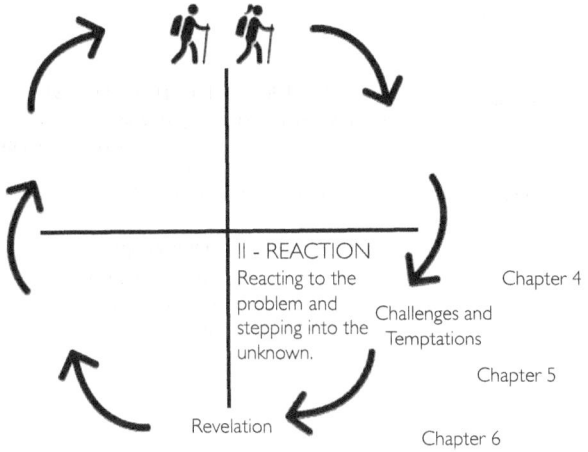

Chapter 4
ATTENTION OVERLOAD

> In Huxley's vision, no Big Brother is required to deprive people of their autonomy, maturity and history. As he saw it, people will come to love their oppression, to adore the technologies that undo their capacities to think
>
> – Neil Postman.

4.1   Limited attention

The purpose of the first act of this book was to make you aware of the level of distraction. Much like the obstacles facing the archetypal hero who is about to undergo a journey, forces of antagonism, or in your case, distraction, are circling around you. Now that you have become conscious of the problem and why it's happening, this second act will start to prepare you for how you can respond to reduce distraction and, ultimately, find your purpose and discover a deeper meaning to life.

I would like you to take a moment and sit back and contemplate the real world wherever you are – the local café where the gruff looking man sits in the corner adding three sugars to his morning tea, or the oak trees that shed their leaves covering the pathway on the street where you live, or the screeching sound coming from the train that runs by overhead. How do you sense and interpret the world of humans and things you encounter? What new understanding do you formulate from observing and being in the world of experiences? What connections can you formulate between things that, on the face of it, might appear disparate? Are you able to somehow join the dots between them?

When we try to break down the setting in which we find ourselves, the outer and the inner, we can soon become overwhelmed by the sheer amount of rich information and experiences around us. It's in these moments, we learn to focus our attention on what's important and ignore the superfluous. Timothy Wilson, a professor of psychology at the University of Virginia, estimates that our brain receives 11 million "bits" of information in the form of sensory experiences each second.[1] Yet despite receiving so much input, our minds can consciously process just 40 bits per second. In other words, the brain is constantly making choices – what chunks of information to process and what to ignore. One way to instruct the choices our mind makes, according to Shawn Achor, author of *The Happiness Advantage* (2010), is to look for positive signals "because the better your brain is at using its energy to focus on the positive, the greater your chances of achieving your goals".[2]

He cites a number of studies that suggest picking up on positive signals can help you make better decisions, be three times more creative, generate 37 per cent more sales, improve your health, increase your productivity by 31 per cent, be 10 times more engaged and 40 per cent more likely to get a promotion. Achor suggests we make a distinction between a signal, something we should pay attention to, and noise, something we should ignore. He explains that information can be identified as noise if it falls into any of the following categories:

- Unusable: The information will not change your behaviour; for example, reading about a natural disaster on the other side of the world, unless you plan to help the victims.
- Untimely: Information that you do not plan to use immediately and may change by the time you use it, such as currency rates for a holiday destination you are going to in six months' time.
- Hypothetical: Where the information is "could be" as opposed to "what is", such as a five-day weather forecast that has a 53 per cent chance of being correct.
- Distracting: In which the information you are receiving distracts you from your career or personal goals. If it does, then it, too, is noise.

When we have limited attention, and need to make a choice between a signal and noise, then directing our mental gaze to what is currently occupying our attentional space becomes crucial; otherwise, we run the risk of senseless mind wandering. Bringing attention to what we are thinking about in the moment is a process called meta-awareness. This is one of the best practices for managing our attention. The more we notice what is occupying our attentional space, the faster we can get back on track when our mind wanders, which it does 47 per cent of the time.

According to Chris Bailey, author of *Hyperfocus* (2018), three combinations of tasks fit comfortably within our attentional space.[3] First, we have minor habitual tasks, like washing the dishes or archiving read emails. We can easily multitask here without impacting the quality of the output. The brain assists us by redirecting blood flow away from the logic centre of the brain, the prefrontal cortex, to the part of the brain that deals with habitual sequences, the basal ganglia.

Secondly, we have a task that needs our focus although it may be a habitual activity. For example, I often listen to a podcast or audiobook whilst doing the ironing. Most of us can comfortably listen to a podcast whilst driving. However, if you are going somewhere unfamiliar and have to read the road signs, it would be more sensible to turn the podcast off in order to allow your brain to focus, or else you could miss your exit. You will also notice that your ability to recall the contents of the podcast is likely to be diminished, as there will have been a significant strain on your short-term memory.

Finally, there are tasks that are complex and require our full attention, and the more effort we exert on them, the better the quality of the output. This could be writing a report, producing a financial model, or running a one-to-one session with one of our team members. We cannot fit two complex tasks into our attentional space simultaneously. The more time and attention we can deploy to a complex task, the greater the impact on productivity and effectiveness.

We often end up trying to do a combination of habitual, focused and complex tasks and end up dropping the ball on at least some if not all of them. Chances are we tried to cram too much into our limited attentional space.

4.2 Packing too much

I know I have had moments when I walked into a room and then forgot why I went there in the first place. You may also have encountered such an episode. I overloaded my mind with too many thoughts vying for my attention, and so didn't have any space left for the original intention. I was thinking about a plot point within a novel, as well as an upcoming social engagement and reminding myself to call a particular family member later in the day. I have found that the best way to avoid this is to be more selective in what is currently occupying my attention. If I am mulling over a plot point within a novel, let me run with that, and if other thoughts pop into my mind, such as a social engagement or the call I need to make, I write these down on my to-do list for the day, so that I can come back to them later on.

Something similar can happen when you commute back from work. Perhaps you are tuned into an audiobook walking back from the train station to your house whilst also reflecting on the events at the office, so much so that you forget to buy bread for the next morning. In order to avoid entering into an autopilot mode, it's best not to allow too many things to pack your attentional space. If you want to listen to the audiobook, then dive deep into the narrative and immerse yourself with the characters. If you want to reflect on the day's events at the office, switch off the audiobook, and think about work. Either way, chances are you will remember to buy the bread on the commute back and not have to go without the next morning.

This type of somnambulant mode, where we are on autopilot, has other drawbacks beyond just forgetfulness. For starters, there is the impact on memory. We read earlier about the experiment that Stanford neuroscientist Russ Poldrack undertook with students studying and watching television at the same time. The information they learned went to the striatum, the wrong part of the brain for recalling later on, when it should have been encoded and catalogued within the hippocampus. I have had occasions where I was watching television whilst surfing around on my smartphone and so had very poor recall as to the contents of what I was actually watching. In fact, the more devices and notifications I have around me, the greater the negative impact on my memory. Technology fast-forwards us, keeps us moving along for the next dopamine hit with some new or novel titbit of insignificant trivia, preventing us from savouring the moment and actually encoding information into our long-term memory.

The danger for us in our professional and personal lives is that we begin ignoring the essential, the critical, the notable and the noteworthy. Maybe we miss a deadline at work, or don't spend time with our children or parents when they need it most. As a West African scholar once said to one of my teachers: "Every step we take in life is one step closer to our death." This should not make us feel morbid and sullen. Rather, it should spur us to make each and every moment count, whether these are moments of individual reflection, meals with family members, conversations with friends, defining periods in our career. If we allow the floodgates of our attention to be overwhelmed and deluged by a river of distraction, then we fail to capture the memories of a time that could have been well-spent but was, instead, scattered into frivolous highlights.

During periods when our attention is overloaded, we feel overwhelmed and are more likely to make mistakes. If we juggle too many things, then we end up paying attention to the highlights, and ignoring the detail. This makes our actions less meaningful and we have poor recall. It's why air traffic controllers land one plane at a time. Otherwise, we are likely to repeat the same mistakes we made in the past. Conversely, when our attentional space is clear and lucid, we also feel uncluttered.

4.3   Unloading the mind

With a gargantuan struggle taking place to distract us, whether this is an external force of antagonism such as the social-media companies, or whether it's our own stray unstructured thoughts, we must recognise that our minds are powerful originators for ideas. However, the more we can get out of our heads, the more clearly we can think. David Allen, author of *Getting Things Done* (2001), says:

> Your head is not for holding ideas—it's for having ideas ... The first thing to do is to capture what's got your attention, then decide if it's actionable or not, and if it is, decide what the next action on it is, and do the action right then if you can.[4]

Allen is referring to the "Zeigarnik effect", named after Bluma Zeigarnik, who, in the late 1920s, stated that incomplete or interrupted tasks weigh on our minds much more than completed tasks. Whenever I think about a task or activity to perform, I write it down in Evernote. As a result, I experience more clarity and less stress. Even if I notice the smallest item weighing on my mind, I externalise it (write it down) to create more attentional space for bigger and better things. The notes app I use (Evernote) syncs between all my devices. My to-do lists are simple: one for work and one for personal matters. However, there are plenty of other possible apps or just a good old-fashioned notebook you can use. The point is: externalise what you are thinking, or else you will forget it.

In *Getting Things Done* (2001), Allen also mentions a "waiting for" list: a list of everything you are waiting on, which – like a to-do list – you should review on a regular basis to make sure nothing slips through the cracks.

From my own experience, the most productive people are the ones who strike a balance between the two extremes, who understand the power of capturing and organising what they have to get done, but who also don't sacrifice real work in favour of being efficient about productivity.

The reality for many knowledge workers is that they need to keep on demonstrating that they are productive members of the organisation, yet what constitutes productivity as a metric is often fuzzy and unclear. To overcome this issue, many knowledge workers resort to how productivity was measured during the Industrial Age, under the Efficiency Movement, founded by Frederick Taylor, who used to stand with a stopwatch in hand measuring the efficiency of worker movements – all the while calculating how to speed up the tasks they were undertaking.

Fast-forward to today's knowledge worker and this manifests itself as a need to be visibly busy and undertaking such mind-and-soul-crushing behaviours as replying to emails immediately no matter what time of day, packing the diary with meetings, many of which are not required, chiming in on Instant Messaging conversations whether they have relevance or not, and firing off random ideas across the office as you walk through – all the while ensuring you are publicly seen to be busy and so, by default, valuable to the organisation. Unfortunately, I have come across a lot of people like this, who give the impression of busyness, yet their work lacks depth, and they do not have the mental discipline to undertake cognitively demanding work.

4.4 Exercise: Impact

Brian Tracy, who wrote the book *Eat That Frog!* (2001), says that "90 per cent of the value that you contribute to your company is contained in [just] three tasks".[5] He recommends a linear process to identify your highest-impact tasks, projects, and commitments. His advice runs as follows:

1. List everything you are responsible for at work. I know you may have a job description, but often what we end up doing varies from how the role was envisaged, so it's a useful exercise to help you recalibrate what you are doing against what you should be doing.
2. What one item on your list is the most valuable and has most impact for your organisation? This is the task you must do day in, day out.
3. Then add a second and third task that you must accomplish within the same period of time that you currently spend on work commitments in your typical day.

You will most likely discover that the three tasks you list most likely make up 15–20 per cent of all your tasks, but they actually contribute 80 per cent of the value you create for your organisation.

Tracy called his book *Eat that Frog!* because he said that if you had to get up in the morning and eat a live frog, it would probably be the hardest thing you would do that day. So the task that is the hardest, we should do first, as once we are done, we will have energy and attentional space for the remainder of the day. Whereas if we put off the hardest task, then it will sap our energy and weigh us down.

4.5 Key points

Some of the critical points we covered in this chapter were as follows:

- Our brain receives 11 million "bits" of information in the form of sensory experiences each second. Yet our minds can consciously process just 40 bits per second. In other words, the brain is constantly making choices, and deciding what chunks of information to process and what to ignore.
- We have limited attention, and need to make a choice between a signal and noise. Directing our mental gaze to what is currently occupying our attentional space becomes crucial. Otherwise, we run the risk of senseless mind wandering.
- Bringing attention to what we are thinking about in the moment is a process called meta-awareness. This is one of the best practices for managing our attention. The more we notice what is occupying our attentional space, the faster we can get back on track when our mind wanders.
- Three combinations of tasks fit comfortably within our attentional space. First, we have minor habitual

tasks, where we can easily multitask. Secondly, we have a task that needs our focus but may also be a habitual activity. Finally, there are tasks that are complex and require our full attention, and the more effort we exert on them, the better the quality of the output.
- During periods when our attention is overloaded, we feel overwhelmed and are more likely to make mistakes. If we end up juggling too many things, we end up paying attention to the highlights, and ignoring the detail.
- The most productive people are the ones who strike a balance and who understand the power of capturing and organising what they have to get done, but who also don't sacrifice real work in favour of being efficient about productivity.

Endnotes

1. *Optimize Your Brain for Success: Reducing Excess and Negative Noise*, Wharton, https://executiveeducation.wharton.upenn.edu/thought-leadership/wharton-at-work/2014/06/reducing-negative-noise.
2. Shawn Achor, *The Happiness Advantage: The Seven Principles of Positive Psychology that Fuel Success and Performance at Work*, Crown Business, 2010.
3. Chris Bailey, *Hyperfocus*, 2018.
4. David Allen, *Getting Things Done*, 2001.
5. Brian Tracy, *Eat That Frog!*, 2001.

Chapter 5
PRACTICES AND HABITS

> As it is not one swallow or a fine day that makes a spring, so it is not one day or a short time that makes a man blessed and happy
>
> – Aristotle.

5.1 Levels

The first part of this act addressed the subject of attention and how we can strengthen our focus to become more present. We are only going to be able to do this when we also possess the belief that we can do this, and this, in turn, starts with habits, as our habits define what becomes routine in our lives. If you want to remove distraction from your life and find your purpose and a deeper meaning to your existence, then you will need to think about altering your habits.

Some years ago when I was involved in grassroots community work, I knew a raucous, rowdy and unruly preacher, who liked to make himself known in every gathering, was opinionated about everything and everyone, and, it seemed to me, his identity was centred on damning all others and informing them how terrible they were. He was not a fellow you would invite to your house for a genial conversation over tea and scones. In fact, over time, I learned to avoid him, particularly in communal gatherings. As the years passed, and I moved for work to other countries, I lost touch with him, but then came across him 10 years later. I recognised him as a person, but I could not recognise the character, the person he had become. Gone was the firebrand hate-monger, and in its place was a gentle soul, utterly humble, modest, devoted to the service of others, showing love and compassion, and whose practices were all about removing the faults from his own self. He was an absolute joy and someone you would certainly invite over for convivial conversation over tea and scones. Hate was a part of his former life, his former identity; love was a part of his current one, his current identity.

When changing our habits, we often try to change the wrong thing. To understand what I am referring to, consider that there are three levels at which change can occur. In his book *Atomic Habits* (2018), James Clear asks us to imagine them like the layers of an onion and calls them outcomes, processes and identity.[1] Other writers go with different labels. For me, the three levels of change are results, practices, and character.

- Results: What is the consequence, the upshot, of what we desire? Perhaps you want to cycle from Vietnam to Cambodia, or learn to play the flamenco guitar, or trek across the Sahara desert. Generally, the targets and ambitions we have in life are aligned with this type of tangible, often measurable and recordable change.
- Practices: The second level of change is about altering our methods, routines and procedures. If you are going to cycle from Vietnam to Cambodia, you will need to instigate a fitness routine to prepare. If you are going to learn to play the flamenco guitar, you will need to understand sheet music or learn with a master. If you are going to trek across the Sahara, you will need to learn how to survive and forage for yourself in a harsh, arid climate. On the whole, the habits we build in life are associated with this level, the practices.
- Character: This is the third and most profound level of change. Here, we get to the heart of who we really are. What do we believe? How do we react in times of crisis? The attitudes, dogmas and convictions we hold are associated with this level. I have to believe I am a cyclist if I am to complete the trip from Vietnam to Cambodia. I have to believe I am a musician in order to learn the flamenco guitar. I have to believe I am an explorer and adventurer to survive the Sahara desert.

When we have a sense of clarity as to our purpose in life, in other words, our character is defined. Then we will institute the correct practices (habits) around us, and we will set realistic and achievable results. Taking one example from above: if I believe I am a musician and this is part of my character, then my daily practices will involve practising the flamenco guitar for at least one hour a day, and the result might be I perform with the flamenco guitar at a family gathering after three months of practice. When we have this clear sense of clarity about our character, then trivial digital distractions simply fade away from our horizons.

5.2 Character-based habits

Unfortunately, we often start our change journey by focusing on the results – that is, the goal – we want to achieve. As a consequence, we gravitate towards building practices (habits) to achieve this result. Yet, until we have truly made a change at the level of character – that is, knowing who we are – our results and practices may be wasted.

Taking some examples mentioned in the previous section, let's break this down a little further for the sake of clarity. Previously, I referred to the following results: cycle from Vietnam to Cambodia, learn to play the flamenco guitar, and trek across the Sahara desert. Let's try to recalibrate the language so that it aligns with our desired character; in other words, who we want to be.

PRACTICES AND HABITS

My purpose in cycling from Vietnam to Cambodia is to become a cyclist. My purpose in learning to play the flamenco guitar is to become a musician. My purpose in trekking across the Sahara desert is to become an explorer. When we set our purpose as becoming a cyclist, a musician, or an explorer, we build the right practices around ourselves to achieve this goal. This might be related to exercising, eating healthily, learning from other musicians, attending concerts, building stamina, or fasting for long periods.

When I first decided to write, I focused on the results (to write a novel) but hadn't put the practices in place (to write 1000 words a day) nor did I have the right attitude or hold true to the conviction to change my character. But when I started to see myself as a novelist and writer, my practices and habits formed around me. My family understood that was who I wanted to be. The results were that I published six novels in six years. Three were self-published, and the other three were published through a conventional publisher.

For too long, I did not commit to writing 1000 words a day of fiction because I didn't believe I was a writer. I always left it for the weekend, or would try to fit it in when I had the time. When I finally started achieving the 1000 words a day, plus bringing in a host of other practices to help me become a writer, then I actually started to form into a new character. We also need to recognise that our character changes as we go through life. What you will be in your 20s, and then 30s, then 40s, will be different. Aside from my daytime job, which paid the bills, in my 20s, I was a community activist. In my

30s, with two young children, I was really just trying to be a parent. It was not until my 40s that I formed a new character, which was that of a novelist and writer.

Remember, you are trying to become the best version of yourself. But who is that person? You must allocate time to reflect and think about this; otherwise, your quest for change will be like a boat without a rudder.

5.3 Improving habits

When we institute practices (habits), it actually provides us with more attentional space and, hence, more time. If we have healthy eating habits, we will have clarity and energy throughout the day. If we have proficient learning habits, we will feel on top of issues and be prepared. If we have prudent financial habits, we will be able to provide for ourselves and our family. Whereas if we are always asking questions of ourselves – "What should I eat?" "What should I read?" "How much should I save every month?" – we end up with less attentional space and time. We are always behind the curve as opposed to moving with the flow.

Practices (habits) develop over time, but there are four simple stages as to how they form in the first place. These are: trigger, urge, action, return.

- Trigger: Something in our environment triggers us to behave in a certain way. We envisage a return. In traditional civilisations, triggers often relate to

matters of food, shelter, cultivation, and safety. For most of us living in developed regions of the world, triggers envisage ancillary returns such as self-gratification, praise, money, friendship, recognition, and reputation.
- Urge: This is the energy behind a habit. It provides the yearning to respond to the trigger. We might not actually desire the habit itself, but we crave the change it brings about. We do not have an urge for coffee in the morning, but we have an urge for the feeling it stimulates, just as we do not have an urge to go to the cinema, but we have an urge to be entertained. Urges will vary across individuals. A glutton, for instance, will have an urge for consumption when a scrumptious platter of food is placed before them, whereas someone who is more in control of their food urges will not have the same level of craving.
- Action: This relates to the actual performance of the habit, such as drinking the cup of coffee you had an urge for in the morning as you walked past the coffee shop on the way to the office and smelt the coffee being brewed, or watching the movie in the cinema for which you saw an advert on your smartphone.
- Return: This is the payoff and the end of the habit – how we felt after drinking the cup of coffee, or watching the movie in the cinema. The trigger alerts us to the return, our urge desires the return, and the action is about acquiring the return. What happened after

the return will also determine whether or not you will be influenced by the trigger when you next encounter it. A glutton who falls prey to a coronary heart attack after stuffing themselves silly for the thousandth time may end up having a life-changing experience and come back months later with more self-restraint and not fall foul of the trigger. They may avoid watching adverts promoting lavish meals, or avoid eating out at shopping malls that are packed with fast-food outlets. They will still be affected by the trigger. They will still have the urge. But if they can avoid the situation, then they are more likely to resist it.

When instilling good practices (habits), we need to make the trigger apparent. For example, if I want to introduce good eating habits, I should ensure there is a bowl of fruit on the table in the kitchen as opposed to a box of chocolates. If someone wants to break their bad habit of playing video games till late in the evening, they should pack up their console and peripherals each evening and store them in a cupboard out of sight. If they do not see the game console (the trigger), they are less likely to have an urge to play games late into the night.

There is also a reframing method we can use to make difficult habits easier by linking them to a positive experience. We often consider habits as things we need to do or are compelled to do. For instance, we need to wake up, we need to cook dinner, we need to call a customer, and we need to compile a weekly report. Let's reframe the word "need" to "opportunity". We have the *opportunity* to wake up and embrace the morning. We have the *opportunity* to cook dinner for our family. We have the *opportunity* to call a customer and deepen our relationship with them. We have the *opportunity* to compile our weekly report so that management are aware of your contribution to the goals of the organisation. The slight reframing of the language can make a huge difference to the attitude we adopt when trying to instil habits that may otherwise prove burdensome.

5.4   Exercise: Three things to do

J. D. Meier, who wrote *Getting Results the Agile Way* (2010), has a method called "the Rule of 3".[2] At the start of each day before you begin work, decide what three things you want to accomplish by the end of the day. Do the same at the start of every week. The three things you identify then become your focus for the day and the week ahead. Here is how to apply the Rule of 3:

1. Write it down: Do not open your email. Instead, take a pen and paper, think about the three things you should have achieved by the end of the day, and write them down. First thing in the morning, before we are confronted with the clutter of electronic communications, our minds are clear and focused.
2. Wins: J. D. Meier suggests the three things you write down are "wins, achievements, or highlights" such as

completing a project milestone, running a successful customer meeting, or clearing your inbox.
3. Schedule: The day before, check your diary so that you know when you have meetings and when you can do your best work without any distraction. Block this time out and also give some thought to where the best location for this work is – a quiet room in the office, a nearby coffee shop, or at home.
4. Minor Tasks: Beyond the three major tasks you have, there will also be some minor tasks that need to be completed. However, these should not be done at the cost of the major tasks.
5. Check-in: Set an alarm, or perhaps two or more in the day, so you can check-in on yourself and remind yourself of the three major tasks you need to accomplish. Confirm you are on track to accomplish these.

5.5 Five-minute instruction

When we try to instil new positive habits, we will inevitably suffer from the apathy of holding onto old decrepit habits that are dragging us down but whose familiarity provides a place within which we can cocoon ourselves and procrastinate to our heart's content. For instance, we keep on picking up our smartphone thinking we just want to quickly check something, but then find we have been sucked into a digital vortex for 30 minutes. Or we keep grazing on snack food like a cow whose head is in a trough, and we find ourselves putting on weight and feeling bloated all day. A time will come in most people's lives when they are ready to make a break from these undesirable habits, and they will throw them out and bring in affirmative habits. Yet, their zeal for the new progressive way of life might also be their undoing, as the person tried to take on too much too soon. They go full-on and find they have actually burned themselves out, and so they fall back into the old familiar and damaging habits instead.

You don't want to do this, and the best way to avoid this is to employ a five-minute instruction to any new helpful habit you want to introduce. In other words, when you start any new habit, cap it at five minutes only. You will be able to sustain the activity for five minutes. See how it goes, then gradually, incrementally, build from there, even if it means adding only one minute extra per week, or every other day.

For instance, when applying the five-minute instruction: reading a book means reading one page; doing a yoga session means doing five minutes of breathing; going for a run means walking for five minutes; meditating and praying means concentrating for five minutes without any other distractions; doing a high-intensity workout means stretching for five minutes. You can apply the five-minute instruction to any habit you want to introduce as it serves as a doorway, making it easier for you to set yourself up for success, and ensure that whatever you do is both sustainable and life-changing in a positive manner.

5.6 Key points

Some of the critical points we covered in this chapter were as follows:

- When changing our habits, we must consider the results (the upshot of what we desire), our practices (our methods, routines and procedures) and our character (who we really are).
- When we have a sense of clarity as to our purpose in life – in other words, our character is defined – then we will institute the correct practices (habits) around us, and we will set realistic and achievable results.
- You are trying to become the best version of yourself. In order to do this, you must allocate time to reflect and think about this; otherwise, your quest for change will be like a boat without a rudder.
- Practices (habits) develop over time, but there are four simple stages as to how they form in the first place. These are: trigger, urge, action, and return.
- When instilling good practices (habits), we need to make the trigger apparent.
- Employ a five-minute instruction to any new helpful habit you want to introduce. In other words, when you start any new habit, cap it at five minutes only and then gradually build it up from there.

Endnotes

[1] James Clear, *Atomic Habits*, 2018.
[2] J. D. Meier, *Getting Results the Agile Way*, 2010.

Chapter 6
ENVIRONMENTAL TRIGGERS

> Be grateful for whoever comes, because each has been sent as a guide from beyond
>
> – Jalaluddin Rumi.

6.1 Environment is key

I once worked for an executive who himself was a fitness freak and was appalled at the junk food eating habits of many of his staff members. Rather than tell them to stop eating processed food, which was most likely going to lead to serious health issues later in life, he began to introduce fruit, vegetable sticks, and other healthy snacks, which were prominently positioned around the office. The catering staff in the office were encouraged to keep the items fresh and well-stocked. He also made sure there were flower bouquets, which created a welcoming atmosphere. Over time, the employees adjusted to this and there were never any fruit or vegetable remaining. Best of all, the odour of junk food no longer permeated like a miasma in the office. The eating and consumption habits of the staff whilst in the office changed.

Our practices change depending on the triggers before us, and the context we find ourselves in leads to the formation of positive or negative practices. If you want to practise the ukulele but you keep it in the guest room, or you want to read a book but the books are kept in a storage box in the garage, then it is simply not going to happen. You are making it really hard for yourself. If your ukulele is right beside your bed, you are more likely to strum it. If the books are on a shelf in your living room, you are more likely to read them. I try to read for at least 20 minutes before falling asleep. I find reading in bed is the trigger for my body to know that it is going to be time to sleep very soon. Obviously, I make sure I have already completed anything I need to do with my smartphone prior to reading.

We can train ourselves to respond to the triggers in the environment around us, which will lead to certain practices. In a study with insomniacs, scientists gave the participants a clear set of instructions that were designed to strengthen the association between the bedroom and sleep, and to re-establish a consistent sleep–wake schedule.[1] They instructed the insomniacs to: go to bed only when sleepy; get out of bed when unable to sleep; use the bedroom for sleep only (no reading, watching TV, etc.); arise at the same time every morning; and don't nap.

The participants in the study began to connect the bedroom with sleep, and for many, it became easier to fall asleep when they went into the bedroom. Of course, other practices were also introduced alongside these instructions, and these related to spending only sleeping time in bed, reducing somatic tension, changing misconceptions about insomnia, and good health practices. The researchers reported:

> The evidence supporting this behavioural approach shows that cognitive-behavioural therapy (CBT) is effective for 70 percent to 80 percent of patients and that it can significantly reduce several measures of insomnia, including sleep-onset latency and wake-after-sleep onset.
>
> Aside from the clinically measurable changes, this therapy system enables many patients to regain a feeling of control over their sleep, thereby reducing the emotional distress that sleep disturbances cause.

6.2   Family and friends

Perhaps one of the most extreme arguments that environmental triggers are able to shape character was promulgated by Laszlo Polgar, a Hungarian man who developed an interesting theory in the 1960s.[2] He believed that: "A genius is not born, but is educated and trained." His view was that, with deliberate practice and the development of good habits, a child could become a genius in any field.

In fact, his convictions were so strong that he decided to test them on his own children. Laszlo and his wife formulated a plan to raise their children to become chess prodigies. To facilitate this, the children were to be home-schooled, which was very unusual in Hungary at the time. The family home was going to be filled with books on chess and pictures of famous chess players.

The couple had three daughters: Susan, Sofia, and Judit. The eldest, Susan, started playing chess as a four-year-old, and within six months, was defeating adults. Sofia was a world champion by 14, and a few years later, became a grandmaster. The youngest, Judit, at 12, was the youngest player ever listed among the top 100 chess players in the world. At 15 years and four months old, she became the youngest grandmaster of all time.[3] In fact, for 27 years, she was the highest-ranked female chess player in the world. The Polgar sisters were raised in an environment where chess was given primacy. Being obsessed with chess was normal in their world.

If you grow up in a family where everyone reads, reading will seem like a desirable thing to do. If you grow up in a family where growing your own food in the garden is part of daily life, you will also regard this as desirable. If you work in an office where people are obsessed with designer clothing brands, then it will also affect your choice of clothes. Either you will go with the flow, or rebel against it.

During the recent COVID-19 pandemic, many people found themselves working from home for long periods of time. Some loved it; others hated it. Much depended on the person's age, their home environment, plus the type of task they were trying to complete. However, being equipped to work from home is not just about having the right technology and broadband available, but also the subtler things that impact our productivity and quality of work. What are the triggers around us? Are we eating healthily by stocking up on non-processed food, which takes longer to break down, sleeping seven to eight hours a day so that our bodies are strong enough to fight off the effects of a virus, and doing regular exercise to boost our mood and build strength?

6.3 Proximity and conformity

Environmental triggers shape our behaviour, as do the people who are in close proximity to us. I worked for an executive who was trigger-happy, ready to declare war on the competition and ruthlessly remove any non-conformist employees. Initially, I found myself being swayed by my boss's character, and I noticed myself becoming less patient and tolerant of others. However, this was not my character, and fortunately, I was able to redress this, and for the staff who worked under both of us, I became a moderating counterweight to his bellicose tendencies.

In the same manner, as we grow up, we learn from our parents about how they manage conflict, and this becomes imbued within our own character. We observe how colleagues get results at work and we tend to follow their example. The collapses of major corporates such as Enron and Worldcom were as much to do with culture as they were to do with financial mismanagement.

One study tracked 12,000 people for 32 years and found that "a person's chances of becoming obese increased by 57 per cent if he or she had a friend who became obese."[4] It works the other way, too. A separate study found that if one person in a relationship lost weight, the other partner would also slim down about one-third of the time.[5] Elsewhere, research suggested that the higher your best friend's IQ at age 11 or 12, the higher your IQ would be at age 15, even after controlling for natural levels of intelligence.[6] The proximity triggers around us seep into our own practices and, ultimately, shape our character.

One of the ways you can enable proximity triggers to start working for you is to identify the character you want to become. What are the traits and behaviours you want to hold? Are you someone who wants to be defined by what you do? Become a writer, a cyclist. Or are you someone who wants to be defined by your actions, to serve others by showing love and compassion? Clearly, it could be both – what you do for yourself and your actions for others. Once you are clear on this, and it will take time, find people who are following those practices. Join a group that has the characteristics you desire. Allow proximity, closeness to them, to trigger the behaviours within you, enabling the right culture, and, ultimately, allow you to become the person you want to be.

ENVIRONMENTAL TRIGGERS

Along with proximity triggers, there is also the matter of conformity and whether we feel compelled to go along with the group. When we have a group where proximity to them is allowing us to become the person we want to be and to seek out the things we value in life, this is a positive scenario. However, we should be mindful that the reverse can also happen – when we inherently disagree with the group but we go along with what they are doing anyway.

One of the classic psychology experiments that demonstrates conformity is from the 1950s and was undertaken by Solomon Asch.[7] Every experiment began in the same way: a subject entered a room with a group of participants who were all strangers. The strangers were actually actors planted by the researcher, and they were instructed to deliver scripted answers to certain questions. The participants were shown one card with a line on it and then a second card with a series of lines. Each person was asked to select the line on the second card that was similar in length to the line on the first card. It was a very simple task.

The length of the line on the first card was clearly the same as Line A. The experiment always started in the same manner, with some easy trials in which all the participants agreed on the correct line. After a couple of rounds, the participants were shown a test that was as simple as the previous ones, but this time, the actors in the room deliberately selected a wrong answer. For example, they would respond "Line C" to the comparison shown in the diagram, even though the answer may have been Line A. All the other actors agreed the lines were the same, even though they were different.

The subject, who is not aware of the deception, becomes puzzled. Eyes opening wide, they begin to laugh nervously to themselves and double-check the reactions of the other participants. Over time, they grow more and more agitated as all the other participants (actors) answer with the incorrect response. After a while, the subject doubts their own eyes, eventually providing an answer they know is wrong.

Asch conducted the experiment in multiple formats, and what he discovered was that as the number of actors increased, so did the conformity of the subject. If it was just the subject and one actor, there was no effect on the person's choice. They just assumed there was something wrong with the other person. When two actors were in the room with the subject, there was still little impact. But as the number of people increased to three actors and four and all the way to eight, the subject became more likely to doubt themselves, and by the end of the experiment, 75 per cent of subjects agreed with the group response even though it was incorrect.

When unsure, we often default to the group. As human beings, we are tuned into what others are doing around us, and the normative view of the majority becomes our standard. As a result, if we want our environment to positively trigger good practices within us, we should encircle ourselves with others who have the practices we want to acquire.

6.4 Priming

The environment around us is critical to how we respond to distraction. Family, friends, proximity and conformity are all triggers. For example, I am sometimes left pondering whether it is my lifelong love of history that resulted in my son choosing to read history at university. And whether it was my impassioned interest in environmental issues since being an undergraduate at the start of the 1990s that resulted in my daughter becoming interested in environmental and animal welfare issues. Of course, both of them would deny such a connection!

Yet, I do puzzle at whether there has been some sort of priming effect, slowly permeating our home environment over the course of a decade, with the use of specific language and ideas that resulted in these practices for my son and daughter. Our home and work environments certainly shape our behaviour, but so do the words and sentences we read and listen to.

The priming impact of words and sentences was particularly heightened during the COVID-19 pandemic, when millions of workers and children were using technology to work and study from home. Their only form of connection with the outside world was via the communications networks and social media that deliver content, be it work-related, news, or entertainment. In this context, what they read and listened to was going to have an impact on their behaviour.

Nobel Prize winner Daniel Kahneman, in his book *Thinking Fast and Slow* (2011),[8] refers to a classic experiment conducted by psychologist John Bargh and his colleagues.[9] They asked students aged 18 to 22 at New York University to construct four-word sentences from a set of five words; for example, "finds", "he", "it", "yellow", and "instantly". One group of students received a scrambled set of words comprising of words associated with the elderly. Being America, these words were "Florida", "forgetful", "bald", "grey", and "wrinkle". In the US, Florida is a well-known location for retirees. After the students finished the task of building out the sentences, they were asked to undertake another experiment in an office down the hall.

Unknown to the students, the actual experiment was the short walk down the corridor. Bargh and his researchers measured the time it took the young participants to get from one end of the corridor to the other. What they found was that the young people who had formulated a sentence from words with an elderly theme walked down the hallway much slower than the others. As Kahneman explains:

> The "Florida effect" involves two stages of priming. First, the set of words primes thoughts of old age, though the word old is never mentioned; second, these thoughts prime a behaviour, walking slowly, which is associated with old age. All this happens without any awareness. When they were questioned afterward, none of the students reported noticing that the words

had had a common theme, and they all insisted that nothing they did after the first experiment could have been influenced by the words they had encountered. The idea of old age had not come to their conscious awareness, but their actions had changed nevertheless. This remarkable priming phenomenon—the influencing of an action by the idea—is known as the ideomotor effect. Although you surely were not aware of it, reading this paragraph primed you as well. If you had needed to stand up to get a glass of water, you would have been slightly slower than usual to rise from your chair—unless you happen to dislike the elderly, in which case research suggests that you might have been slightly faster than usual.

Reciprocal links are common in the associative network. For example, being amused tends to make you smile, and smiling tends to make you feel amused. Go ahead and take a pencil, and hold it between your teeth for a few seconds with the eraser pointing to your right and the point to your left. Now hold the pencil so the point is aimed straight in front of you, by pursing your lips around the eraser end. You were probably unaware that one of these actions forced your face into a frown and the other into a smile. College students were asked to rate the humour of cartoons from Gary Larson's *The Far Side* while holding a pencil in their mouth. Those who were "smiling" (without any awareness of doing so) found the cartoons funnier than did those who were "frowning." In another experiment, people whose face was shaped into a frown (by squeezing their eyebrows together) reported an enhanced emotional response to upsetting pictures—starving children, people arguing, maimed accident victims.

The general theme of these findings is that the idea of money primes individualism: a reluctance to be involved with others, to depend on others, or to accept demands from others. The psychologist who has done this remarkable research, Kathleen Vohs, has been laudably restrained in discussing the implications of her findings, leaving the task to her readers. Her experiments are profound—her findings suggest that living in a culture that surrounds us with reminders of money may shape our behaviour and our attitudes in ways that we do not know about and of which we may not be proud.

During the global lockdown, many workers took to checking the news regularly to see how apocalyptic things were and how much worse they were going to get. As someone conveyed to me during that time: "We don't know when this will end, or if this is the end." Whatever the future holds, we should try to ensure the environment we exist within, whether it is the workplace or home, is priming us in a positive manner, where we avoid distraction, focus on what we value, and are generous towards others by being in their service.

6.5 Implementation intention

In a crisis, we come to a turning point. We have to decide. Choose. It is this intensity that makes it feel like a crunch moment, and this is because humans have a natural affinity with the status quo. Very few of us like change. During the global lockdown, which started in 2020, home-working went from a nice-to-have to a must-have. The World Economic Forum estimated that pre-COVID-19, only 7 per cent of US workers regularly worked from home, and in Europe, it was around 25 per cent.[10] Many organisations regarded home-working as a benefit only available for senior executives and some knowledge workers. All that changed.

Where home-working or hybrid-working is an option for employees and managers to offer, setting clear intentions about when, where and how they will work from home and when, where, and how they will fit their personal lives around their work will be critical. Without this, the best of efforts can go to waste for both the employee and the wider organisation.

Researchers in the UK worked with a group to build better exercise habits over the course of two weeks.[11] The subjects were divided into three groups. The first group was the "control" group. They were asked to track how often they exercised. The second group was the "motivation" group. They were asked to track their workouts but also to read some material on the benefits of exercise. The researchers explained to the motivation group how exercise could reduce the risk of coronary heart disease and improve heart health.

Finally, there was the third group. They received the same presentation as the second group, which ensured they had equal levels of motivation. They were given the following written instruction: "Many people find that they intend to take at least one 20-minute session of vigorous exercise but then forget or 'never get around to it'. It has been found that if you form a definite plan of exactly when and where you will carry out an intended behaviour you are more likely to actually do so and less likely to forget or find you don't get round to doing it. It would be useful for you to plan when and where you will exercise in the next week."

Specifically, each member of the third group completed the following sentence: "During next week, I will partake in at least 20 minutes of vigorous exercise on (day or days)_____ at _____(time of day) at/or in (place)_____."

In the first and second groups, 35 to 38 per cent of people exercised at least once per week. But in the third group, who made the clear intention, 91 per cent exercised at least once a week. The sentence they filled out is what researchers refer to as an implementation intention, which is a plan you make beforehand about when and where to act.

When you set an implementation intention it makes a huge difference to ensuring you actually carry out what you intended. This is really important for well-being as the boundary between work and home life blurs. For example, if you want to stop working on your day job at 6pm, then make an implementation intention that goes something like this: "Switch my work mobile to flight mode at 6pm." Or if you find you aren't getting to sleep at the right time, make an implementation intention like: "Set an alarm for 9:30pm, turn off all electronic devices and start winding down." Remember medical research demonstrates that sleep boosts your immunity, which is really helpful at the best of times, and vital during the worst.[12]

6.6 Firmer intentions

Imagine for a moment that you have made some implementation intentions so that you can focus on what really matters in life. Perhaps they are something like this:

1. Go cycling this weekend.
2. Practise the guitar.
3. Get to sleep at a sensible time.

Research by Peter Gollwitzer found that even vague intentions like these boost your odds of successfully carrying them out by around 20–30 per cent. However, when we set more specific intentions, the chances, according to one study done by Gollwitzer, rise to 62 per cent. He says that:

> When people encounter problems in translating their goals into action (e.g. failing to get started by becoming distracted or falling into bad habits), they may strategically call on automatic processes in an attempt to secure goal attainment. This can be achieved by

plans in the form of implementation intentions that link anticipated critical situations to goal-directed responses ("Whenever situation x arises, I will initiate the goal-directed response y!"). Implementation intentions delegate the control of goal-directed responses to anticipated situational cues, which (when actually encountered) elicit these responses automatically.[13]

Whether you consider the 62 per cent of the Gollwitzer study or the 91 per cent from the UK study, the point is that when you set an implementation intention, it makes a huge difference to ensuring you actually carry out what you intended.

Let us return to the vague intention I mentioned a couple of paragraphs up and re-write these:

1. "Go cycling this weekend" becomes "Diary a 30-minute cycle ride on Saturday at 8am."
2. "Practise the guitar" becomes "Practise the guitar straight after work from 6pm for 30 minutes."
3. "Get to sleep at a sensible time" becomes "Set a bedtime alarm for 9pm and start winding down."

Whenever I find my time in the evening being eroded by trivia, I resort back to setting a bedtime alarm for 9pm. This signals to me that I need to be in bed by around 9:30pm, with a view to reading for 20 minutes and getting to sleep by 10pm. As I wake up around 5:45am, this provides me with the requisite amount of sleep my body needs to function throughout the day.

All of this hinges on two factors. Firstly, you have to actually care about your intentions. Secondly, implementation intentions work better with more difficult tasks that you might otherwise procrastinate over.

6.7   Diderot effect

The Chief Editor and co-founder of the Encyclopédie in the 18th century was the French philosopher Denis Diderot (1713–1784). Disowned by his father after he gave up a career in law to become a writer, he lived a bohemian, poverty-soaked existence for most of his life. When it came time for his daughter to marry, he could not afford to pay for her wedding.

Upon hearing of this tribulations, Catherine the Great, Empress of Russia and admirer of the Encyclopédie, offered to buy Diderot's personal library for 50,000 francs and asked Diderot to become her personal librarian, a position for which he undertook, much to his displeasure as he did not like to travel, a journey to Russia.

This enabled Diderot to finance his daughter's wedding, but he also purchased a scarlet robe for himself. He greatly loved the robe and soon realised that his other more common belongings, such as his chair, desk, rug, and other household items, looked out of place beside the lavish robe. He swapped his rug with one from Damascus. He decorated his home with expensive sculptures. He purchased a mirror to place above the mantel, and a superior kitchen table. He threw away his Spartan straw chair for a plush Moroccan leather one. One purchase led to the next, connecting together in a spiral of consumption.

In fact, this phenomenon, where obtaining a new possession creates a spiral of consumption that leads to additional purchases, is known as the Diderot Effect. We recognise this because we have all done it. You buy a new armchair and then question the compatibility of the sofa you already have in the living room. Or you buy a new dress and have to acquire new shoes and earrings to go with it. In other words, there is a chain reaction of purchases, in which one leads to another.

The same is true of practices and ways of working. It takes about one month for new work habits and routines to bed-in. During the global lockdown, depending on where you were located, many people took to going for a quick walk during the day, or doing a fifteen-minute, high-intensity workout between conference calls, or taking time to reflect in solitude over the morning tea of coffee. These are all positive practices. One way of retaining these is to link or cascade them with other good habits, a sort of positive Diderot Effect, where we have a chain reaction of practices that will help us become the person we want to be. The next exercise will offer some suggestions as to how this can be implemented at a more practical level.

6.8 Exercise: Building habits

One way of institutionalising practices (habits) is to connect them with other positive ones, where one leads to another, which leads to another. This system, known as habit stacking, was developed by B. J. Fogg as part of his *Tiny Habits* program.[14] The habit stacking formula is: "After [current habit], I will [new habit]."

For example:

- Reflection. After I drink a cup of tea in the morning, I will reflect for two minutes.
- Fitness. After closing my laptop at 6pm, I will immediately change into my fitness clothes.
- Gratitude. When I get to bed, I will think about all the things I am grateful for in my life.

Obviously, you can tie more than two habits together. Habit stacking enables you to create a set of rules to guide your future behaviour. Here are some more general habit stacks as a guide:

- Nutrition. When I wake up in the morning, I will first drink a glass of water.
- Environment. When I take a flight, I will offset my carbon by organising for a tree to be planted.
- Finances. When I want to buy something expensive, I will donate a small amount of money to charity.
- Minimalism. When I buy a new set of clothes, I will give an old set to charity.
- Gratefulness. When something good happens to me, I will think about the people less well off than me and do something for them.

6.9 Key points

Some of the critical points we covered in this chapter were as follows:

- Our practices change depending on the triggers before us, and the context we find ourselves in leads to the formation of positive or negative practices.
- We can train ourselves to respond to the triggers in the environment around us, which will lead to certain practices.
- Environmental triggers shape character. If you grow up in a family where everyone reads, reading will seem like a desirable thing to do. If you grow up in a family where growing your own food in the garden is part of daily life, you will also regard this as desirable.
- Proximity triggers around us (e.g. the people we spend time with) seep into our own practices and, ultimately, shape our character.
- When unsure, we often default to the group. As human beings, we are tuned into what others are doing around us, and the normative view of the majority becomes our standard.
- We can be primed by a set of words that generate certain thoughts, which then prime a behaviour, such as in the Florida Effect.
- An implementation intention makes a huge difference to ensuring you actually carry out what you intended.

- Even vague intentions boost your odds of successfully carrying out what you intended by 20–30 per cent. However, when you set more specific intentions, the chances rise to 62–91 per cent (depending on different studies).
- One way of institutionalising practices (habits) is to connect them with other positive ones, where one leads to another, which leads to another – a positive Diderot Effect.

Endnotes

1. Charles M. Morin, "Psychological and Behavioural Treatment of Insomnia: Update of the Recent Evidence (1998-2004)", *Sleep*, vol. 29, no. 11, 2006.
2. Lazlo Polgar, *Bring up Genius!*, 1989.
3. Judit Polgar, *How I Beat Fischer's Record*, 2012.
4. Nicholas A. Christakis and James H. Fowler, "The Spread of Obesity in a Large Social Network over 32 Years", *New England Journal of Medicine*, 357, no. 4, 2007.
5. Amy A. Gorin et al., "Randomised Controlled Trial Examining the Ripple Effect of a Nationally Available Weight Management Program on Untreated Spouses", *Obesity*, 26.
6. Ryan Meldrum, Nicholas Kavish and Brian Boutwell, "On the Longitudinal Association between Peer and Adolescence Intelligence: Can Our Friends Make Us Smarter?", *PsyArXiv*, Feb 2018.
7. S. E. Asch, "Effects of group pressure on the modification and distortion of judgments", In H. Guetzkow (ed.), *Groups, leadership and men*, Pittsburgh, PA, Carnegie Press, 1951, pp. 177-190.
8. Daniel Kahneman, *Thinking Fast and Slow*, 2011.
9. John A. Bargh, Mark Chen and Lara Burrows, "Automaticity of social behaviour: direct effects of trait construct and stereotype-activation on action", *Journal of Personal Social Psychology* 71, 1996, pp. 230-44.

10 World Economic Forum https://www.weforum.org/agenda/2020/03/working-from-home-coronavirus-workers-future-of-work/.

11 Sarah Milne, Sheina Orbell and Paschal Sheeran, "Combining Motivational and Volitional Interventions to Promote Exercise Participation", *British Journal of Health Psychology* 7, May 2002, pp. 163-184.

12 NHS, https://www.nhs.uk/live-well/sleep-and-tiredness/why-lack-of-sleep-is-bad-for-your-health/.

13 Peter Gollwitzer, "Implementation Intentions: Strong Effects of Simple Plans", *The American Psychologist*, Vol. 54, 7, 1999, pp. 493-503.

14 B. J. Fogg, *Tiny Habits*, 2019.

ACT III

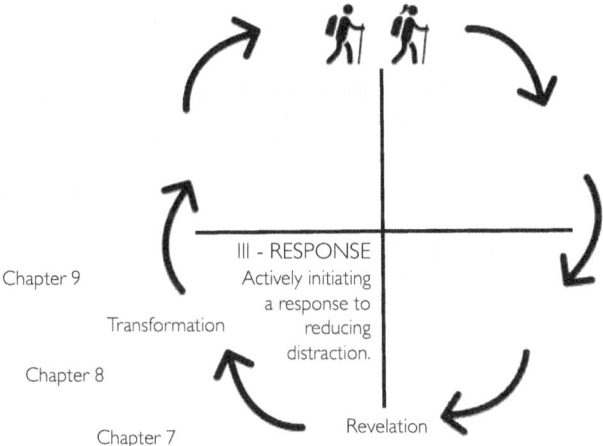

ACT III

Chapter 7
MINIMISING DISTRACTION

> You have power over your mind – not outside events. Realise this, and you will find strength
>
> – Marcus Aurelius.

7.1   What is necessary

In Act I, we became aware of the level of distraction around us, and how the forces of antagonism are taking us away from thinking about our true purpose, if we even had time to identify what it might be. Act II followed up by looking at how we can react to this problem by managing our attention, habits and the environment we choose to place ourselves in. Now we move into Act III, where we begin to actively initiate a response to the problem. This act is all about countering the problem of distraction now that you are more familiar with the territory you find yourself in.

One piece of knowledge I repeat time and again when people ask me about my own productivity and time management journey is that the path is not linear. We all have times in life when we fall back into bad habits, we procrastinate, and we are not very productive. This happens to me quite often, and I have to remind myself not to be distracted, to focus on what I value most, and reset my journey towards what my true purpose in life is. This is simply part of what it means to be human, so don't be too hard on yourself when you fall back into bad habits. Rather, be mindful you have reversed, re-set yourself, and then move forward once more.

One way to gain momentum towards what you should be doing is to pay attention to what is necessary. It is not about how much you do, but it is about doing the right things, the necessary things.

Throughout my career, I have rarely taken on a project or task without first reflecting on whether it is something I can truly provide value on and whether it is something I can do with excellence. More often than not, my default position is no – I refuse the work. This has enabled me to be selective about my work and produce high-quality deliverables.

7.2 Achievers irony

One of the outcomes of the COVID-19 pandemic was that it facilitated thoughtful business leaders to ask existential questions about purpose and priorities in their work and personal lives. No one but a fanatical few wants to return to a normal in which they run the serious possibility of burning themselves and their employees out. Doing so not only harms the employee, but the dependent families who are always short of a member of the household – there is a long-term impact on the development of children and wider implications for society. All this is conveniently off balance-sheet externalities for some unscrupulous employers, who simply are not prepared to look at the strain they place on employees.

For individuals who want to be successful at work but also have a purposeful life away from the office, here lies the dilemma of attainment. For if we do not prioritise our lives, someone else will, and life will play out in the following way:

- Stage 1: We begin by working hard to accomplish what we set out to do and are clear about our purpose and priorities, and it is this clarity that leads to our attainment.
- Stage 2: We become known as a fixer, someone who has a reputation for getting things done, and so we are offered further openings and opportunities.
- Stage 3: However, these additional openings and opportunities create strains on our time and energy and our efforts become dispersed as we get stretched.
- Stage 4: We are seriously distracted from what should have been the most important priority. As a result, we undercut the clarity that resulted in our attainment in the first place, and this leads to our burning out and crashing.

DISTRACTING OURSELVES TO DEATH

Greg McKeown, author of *Essentialism* (2014), says that: "Success can distract us from focusing on the essential things that produce success in the first place." He further adds:

> The word priority came into the English language in the 1400s. It was singular. It meant the very first or prior thing. It stayed singular for the next five hundred years. Only in the 1900s did we pluralise the term and start talking about priorities.
>
> Illogically, we reasoned that by changing the word we could bend reality. Somehow, we would now be able to have multiple "first" things. People and companies routinely try to do just that.[1]

Of course, the implication of this is that we learn to say no more often, but that is not a bad thing because it means we can focus on the priorities that fulfil our purpose. As a result, we should be asking ourselves: what challenge do I want to work on and what do I want to spend my limited time on?

I have had moments in my career where I said no to bosses because the request was taking me away from the central purpose of my role and, so, the success of the organisation. I remember one boss who had a "special project" that he wanted me to take a look at when I had a moment. I did not have a moment, unless I was prepared to give up vast hours of my weekend for the next two months. I assessed the "opportunity" and decided against it. My boss was not impressed and found a peer of mine who did take on the "challenge", with the result that my peer burnt themselves out, resented the manager for giving them the special project and found an opportunity outside the organisation. We all know the tremendous cost involved in recruitment and retention, so to bleed talent out in this way is a violation of the commitments we make to our employers.

As the late Peter Drucker, a management thinker, said:

> In a few hundred years, when the history of our time will be written from a long-term perspective, it is likely that the most important event historians will see is not technology, not the internet, not e-commerce.
>
> It is an unprecedented change in the human condition. For the first time – literally – substantial and rapidly growing numbers of people have choices. For the first time, they will have to manage themselves. And society is totally unprepared for it.[2]

Drucker is right – the majority of people have not asked themselves what their purpose in life is, what they want to spend their limited time on, and what they should avoid. Ultimately, the hopeful message is that we can all prepare by asking ourselves a very simple question – What is necessary? – and then choose to ignore everything else.

7.3 Digital restraint

Perhaps one of the strongest forces of antagonism that is distracting us from purpose in our professional working lives as well as our personal lives is the ubiquitous rise of purposeless non-essential digital technologies. Please do not misunderstand me here. Digital technologies have a place – if they help us fulfil our purpose. As a writer, I am indebted to my laptop and software, and any amateur cyclist who competes will tell you they are heavily reliant on their tracking and performance apps. I am not talking about the types of digital technologies that augment your purpose in life. Rather, I am referring to the ones we encountered in Act I – particularly social media, where dopamine is used to keep us jacked into an endless cycle of frivolous entertainment.

Cal Newport, author of *Digital Minimalism* (2019), argues that what we need is a:

> Full-fledged philosophy of technology use, rooted in your deep values, that provides clear answers to the questions of what tools you should use and how you should use them and, equally important, enables you to confidently ignore everything else.[3]

Newport forcefully makes the case that we should spend our online time on a few carefully chosen activities that support the things we value, and gladly miss out on all others. In other words, ask the question "What do I really value?" and then determine how technology can supplement this value. Technology should be there to support the thing you value. It is not the source of value in and of itself, unless you happen to be a technology geek. Then, fine, – go do your thing. If you are a gardener, use carefully selected technology to become a better gardener. Likewise, if you are a musician, use technology to make you a better artist.

Newport's philosophy rests on the following three principles:

- Principle 1 – Clutter is costly: Littering our time and attention with too many devices, apps, and services results in a negative cost that drowns the small benefits that each individual item provides in isolation.
- Principle 2 – Optimisation is important: To unlock the benefit of a technology, think carefully about how to use it.
- Principle 3 – Intentionality is satisfying: When we are more intentional about how we use technology, it leads to significant satisfaction about how we engage with technology.

Minimising, decluttering, stripping out distraction, allows us to have clear space for reflection. It's the very thing the social-media companies and those whose business models are built on grabbing our attention don't want us to do. And, ironically, it's the very thing we need to do if we are going to escape the gravitational pull of frivolous distractions in our life.

7.4 Applying it

If one way of minimising distraction is to focus on what is necessary, ignoring everything else, as well as showing digital restraint and only using technology that helps us fulfil our purpose, then how can we actually apply this in the work settings within which we find ourselves?

As our goal is to focus on necessary work, let's create two categories to help us consider this further: work that is vital and work that is optional. In an applied sense, this means the following:

- Vital work: This is what we are paid to do. If you are a salesperson, this will be to close deals; a financial advisor, to manage the portfolio of your client; a consultant, to advise your client. If you can stay in this zone, then you are providing value to the organisations you work for and are being productive in what you do. There will always be a subset of vital work, which, depending on your character, may be uninviting to do, such as attending budget meetings, doing mandatory training, or writing monthly reports. These uninviting tasks should not take more than 20 per cent of our time and effort, or else we run the risk of losing sight of our main purpose. This same formula can be applied to our personal lives. As a parent, a vital task is giving time to your children and providing a nurturing environment. Uninviting tasks may be cleaning out the mess young junior left after his morning meal came back up – but as any parent will tell you, this goes with the territory.
- Optional work: These are all tasks that fall outside the vital, as we do not accomplish much by doing them

compared to our vital tasks. For example, tidying up our inbox, clearing out paperwork from the office, reading the newspaper for the fifth time that morning. Generally, we gravitate towards these tasks when we dawdle over doing something else that may be uninviting, such as completing the annual mandatory health-and-safety training, which is overdue. In our personal lives, we can find ourselves stuck in a loop of optional tasks, such as browsing on our smartphones, when there are more vital tasks to be done. We feel busy because of the dopamine hits we are getting, but deep down, we know we are not fulfilling our purpose in life and the clock is ticking.

When we start something new like a job, or move into a new home, we seem to have a clearer line of sight into what is vital and what is optional, whereas over time, this becomes a little fudged. It's a really useful exercise to do every few months, to recalibrate yourself by asking what is vital and what is optional in both your professional working life and your personal one.

7.5 Exercise

Considering the ideas we have covered in this chapter, such as what is necessary, achievers irony, and digital restraint, use the following table to write down what is vital and what is optional within your working life and your personal life.

I am using working and personal as two broad categories. You may choose to use other labels, such as professional, business, home, and so on.

	Working Life	**Personal Life**
VITAL		
OPTIONAL		

7.6 Key points

Some of the critical points we covered in this chapter were as follows:

- One way to gain momentum towards what you should be doing is to pay attention to what is necessary. It is not about how much you do, but it is about doing the right things, the necessary things.
- If we do not prioritise our lives, someone else will.
- When we learn to say no more often, it means we can focus on the priorities that fulfil our purpose.
- The majority of people have not asked themselves what their purpose in life is, what they want to spend their limited time on, and what they should avoid.

- We should spend our online time on a few carefully chosen activities that support the things we value, and gladly miss out on all others.
- Minimising, decluttering, and stripping out distraction allows us to have clear space for reflection.
- To help focus on what is necessary, create two categories: work that is vital and work that is optional.

Endnotes

1. Greg McKeown, *Essentialism*, 2014.
2. Peter Drucker, "Managing Knowledge Means Managing Oneself", *Leader to Leader Journal*, no. 16, Spring 2000.
3. Cal Newport, *Digital Minimalism*, 2019.

Chapter 8
OPERATING MODES

> One who knows others is clever, but one who knows himself is enlightened. One who conquers others is powerful, but one who conquers himself is mighty
>
> — Lao Tzu.

8.1 Dealing with distractions

In the previous chapter, we looked at ways to minimise distraction. We will now extend this further and start to address our operating modes and rhythms at work – how we get stuff done in a typical day. As a result, this chapter will be full of small but useful productivity hacks, which, if you can implement, will create an incremental improvement in removing distraction from your life and allowing you the time to find purpose and meaning.

Fortunately, most of the distractions in life can be constrained. This is a hopeful position to start from. It is within our ability to show restraint in matters to do with: email, phone alerts, meetings, social media, news websites, and messaging applications. Despite the sophisticated software engineering of the major technology firms tapping into our brains and stimulating them to release dopamine, if we really show self-control, it is within our ability to minimise and, if required, totally eliminate these distractions.

There are also other distractions that are outside our influence and sway. These might be an impromptu coffee meeting, a conversation in the canteen, a call from a friend or family member when working on a document, a loud colleague sitting close by you in the office, or a visitor who shows up unexpectedly. In these cases, it's best to just go with the flow, enjoy the moment and then return to what you were doing later on.

8.2   Operating at depth

Everyone's role will entail some level of cognitively demanding work or, as Cal Newport calls it, "Deep Work". This might be 90 per cent of the role if your job is to create intellectual capital, or it might be 10 per cent if you are sitting in a contact centre receiving inbound voice calls from customers. For me, cognitively demanding work entails: writing or researching and thinking about a business problem, writing a paper, or crunching through a financial model. When I am doing any of these tasks, I need to metaphorically hold my breath and dive deep like a traditional pearl diver, for I know it's only when I get to a certain level of cognitive depth that I will discover the jewels I am searching for. At this deep depth, I can make the connections that I couldn't discern whilst swaying about in the shallows. For others, cognitively demanding work may include: writing a human resources policy, preparing a strategy presentation, or architecting a complex project plan. Depending on the nature of your job, this will vary.

The point here is that when you are in this mode, you want to avoid distractions at all costs. Remember it takes about 25 minutes to return to the same level of cognitive depth you were at before you got distracted. As a professional in a highly competitive world, you simply cannot afford to waste time being distracted by the frivolous and trivial. As a result, here are some broad suggestions about how to avoid becoming distracted when you need to undertake cognitively demanding work:

- Do not disturb. Depending on the working culture within your organisation and the level of acceptance to this, try to activate "do not disturb" for periods of time. You can do this by moving into an empty meeting room and putting up a sign, switching your messaging application to this mode, or making your online presence offline. If you have an open-plan office, then make an agreement with your colleagues, and when they see a sign on your desk indicating that you should not be disturbed, then you should not be.

This signal could be a small lamp that you switch on when you do not want to be disturbed, or a sign that you hang up. I would suggest you try with small bite-sizes of do-not-disturb time first, say 30 minutes. See how you go, and you can build it up from there to whatever the needs of your work are. You will be surprised how much you can get done when your mind is free from incoming messages and notifications.

- Block incoming notifications. If you find it difficult to restrain yourself from checking your social media and email, then take the decision out of your hands and install an app that blocks all websites for a period of time. This way, even if you have the urge to check, you cannot do so. Closing down the Wi-Fi on your computer or unplugging it from the Ethernet cable will also have the same result. If you take your laptop with you to a coffee shop or another location where you need to get deep work done, ask yourself whether you really need to be online. If you don't, then don't request the Wi-Fi password from the barista.
- Cancel the noise. The trend to open-plan offices over the past two decades has resulted in a cacophony of noise reverberating around offices. It's easier to concentrate when the background noise all melds into one, but if we start to pick up distinct conversations, we become distracted. In such a situation, investing in noise-cancelling headphones will help, or if you do not want that financial outlay, then simply use some earbuds to block out the noise.

- Work remotely. Prior to the COVID-19 pandemic, many employers were neutral to unsupportive about their employees being out of the office. They wanted facetime, to see their staff sitting at the desk. However, post-COVID, the culture has changed. If you are able, take yourself out of the office for periods of time, into a coffee shop or another location, where you will not be disturbed and you can dive into the work.

One significant benefit I have had from removing distraction when I have cognitively demanding work is that I can maintain my energy levels for much longer. I feel less drained because I am not spending time jumping around from one thing to the next, with cortisol and adrenaline firing off. The quality of our work is dependent on how much we concentrate and for how long we can concentrate.

8.3 Operating in the shallows

There will be times, maybe most of the time depending on the role you perform, when you don't need to submerge yourself in cognitively demanding work, but you can, instead, float around in the shallows. Even if you occupy this space, you still need to be able to manage your distractions so that they don't overwhelm you. Here are some practical tips to manage distraction in the shallows:

Notifications. Before realising there was a feature on my smartphone that could disable notifications from text messages, social media, messaging applications and the like, I would, like a conditioned human version of Pavlov's dogs, pick up my phone and check the notification. Or if I was on my work laptop, I would be drawn into the notification or IM that just went off and, as we learned earlier, reduce my effective IQ by 10 points. I then decided to turn off all notifications other than SMS, which sends out a mini-vibration. I felt a lot better and can now go through long periods, up to 45–60 minutes, concentrating deeply. Try to turn off all but the very necessary notifications on your phone. Some of you may have older parents or younger children who may need to contact you in an emergency. Others will be in jobs where there are certain VIP-type customers who expect to get a response immediately. With smartphones nowadays you can easily set an override if certain people reach out to you.

Smartphones. It's amazing how much we lean on our smartphones like crutches, supporting us through the day, glued in our hands, like modern-day prayer beads. Yet, unlike the latter, this technological piece of wizardry is chewing away at our souls. There are certain occasions in the day when I would urge you to stop your smartphone from running and ruining your life, such as numb moments – when we tend to be waiting around for something to happen, like when we are in a long queue or waiting for a train to arrive. Next time this happens, avoid activating your smartphone. Instead, reflect and ponder on the day. Consider certain aspects of your life and how you can improve them. Really think hard about what value the apps on your phone are bringing to your life. Do you really need them? If not, delete them, or shift them to a page or folder in your smartphone that you rarely visit. If the smartphone remains within sight, you will be tempted to pick it up. When I need to work on something important, I tend to keep my smartphone a couple of meters away from me and outside my vision.

Email. This is very challenging for most people. Remember the study we mentioned earlier about effective IQ dropping by 10 points when participants could see there was an email notification waiting for them? If we add up this IQ loss across an organisation, that is a lot of intellectual capital leaking out. Over the years, there have been numerous publications that address the hidden cost to an organisation due to an overzealous email culture. One such study was reported in *Harvard Business Review* by Tom Cochran, then CTO of Atlantic Media.[1] He measured that in a single week, he received 511 email messages and sent 284. This averaged to around 160 emails per day over a five-day week. Assuming he only spent 30 seconds per message on average, this accumulated to an hour and a half per day dedicated to moving information around like a sorting machine. Delving deeper, he found that Atlantic Media was spending well over a million dollars a year to pay people to process emails.

Whether you attempt to do such a calculation for your own organisation will depend on how bad the email culture is, but the point to underline is that there is a hidden impact to your bottom line. Some of the techniques I use to manage email are as follows:

- Schedule when I check email. This tends to be in the morning, lunchtime and then towards the end of the day. All other times, the email client on my laptop remains closed. If it's urgent, someone will call me. Now, I appreciate that if you are working on a tight deadline, with a tender submission due within 24–48 hours, then, of course, this is not possible, and I don't follow this practice either. However, for the regular working day, you can implement this or another routine. Perhaps checking email three times a day is not doable in your role, so instead think about checking every two hours, or if you really need to, then on the top of every hour. Fire up the email, set a 10-minute counter, and then stop when the time runs out, and return to the main focus of your work. Answering email is shallow logistical work, which will most likely be done by machine learning algorithms within a decade, so the sooner you realise that responding to email is not cognitively demanding work that creates value for your organisation, the better it will be for you in the long-term.

- Sprint through. I often set myself a countdown timer for 15, 20 or 30 minutes and then power through as many emails as possible, and stop when the timer counts to zero. My work inbox normally does not have more than 20–30 emails in it. Either I have filed or responded to them. You will be surprised how many emails you can sprint through when you set a countdown timer for yourself. Only come back to them when you next check emails.
- Separate to-do list. My to-do list is not on any application within my email client. That way, there is no

temptation to get sucked into the vortex of incoming emails. I use OneNote at work and Evernote at home, but there are plenty of other good applications out there that you can select.
- Brevity. Learn to keep the emails you write short and to the point. No one wants to receive a thesis on email. Four to five sentences should be the maximum, with a clear call to action. Is this for information? Do you want a decision from the person you are sending the message to? Or would you like them to respond, and, if so, by when? Also after you have drafted the email, re-read it a couple of times, polishing the language and ensuring there is no room for misunderstanding.
- Emotive topics. When I receive an email on an emotive topic, which for whatever reason has annoyed or frustrated me, I never respond immediately. I allow myself time to think so that I can respond in a pragmatic and measured manner. Sometimes I will even go for a short walk to let off steam. I think about all the things I am grateful for in my life and come back in a better frame of mind.
- Boundaries. I do not check emails after working hours or on the weekends, and definitely never when I am on holiday. Depending on the nature of your work and the expectations within your organisation, you may or may not be able to implement this. However, there will certainly be some times when you can set a boundary and tell yourself and your line manager that you will not check emails. One study showed

that being expected to monitor work email on a 24/7 basis took a toll on the mental health and well-being of both the employee and their partner (a spill-over effect).[2] These employees also reported higher levels of anxiety. What was startling was that negative effect was not linked to how long they spent on their work emails; it was actually linked to the expectation of being online and available to respond to emails.

Meetings. These can take up much of the day if you are not careful. I always question why I am attending a meeting. Can I add value to it, or is it for information only, such as a briefing from senior executives? When I send out an invite for a meeting, I always include a sentence starting with "Purpose of the Meeting". The invitees must know why they are spending their and the organisation's valuable time speaking with me. Here are a couple of tips for meetings:

- Purpose or agenda. If it is not clearly stated, then push back to the organiser and ask for this clarification. Likewise, if you are the organiser, let attendees know. If it is a significant decision-making meeting, you must include a detailed agenda as well as outline the key decisions that need to be made, such as a decision related to an investment, an office opening or closure, and so on.
- Recurring meetings: If you are regularly going to spend your time on a set of meetings, be very clear about what value you can offer. If you can't, then question why you are attending.

- Attendees: Be sure to have the right people at the meeting, so that you don't need to repeat it in the future because the decision-makers were not there. Who can make decisions, who are the influencers, what facts and information will be presented, what choices need to be made, and what considerations need to be taken into account? If it is a really important meeting, I always hold one-on-one sessions with the key decision-makers in the week prior to the main meeting. That way, I can ensure there are no surprises for them at the meeting, they know what they are being asked to decide and I can fathom their opinions and adjust anything that might be required. Senior decision-makers will always appreciate you taking this extra step, as they will feel more included in the decision-making process. It also ensures the main forum runs more smoothly as everyone is already on-board. Many years ago, I worked in a department where once a month a major all-day, face-to-face meeting involving 20–30 participants was held, in which product managers would be invited to articulate why their products were "worthy" of being launched through the channel marketing team into the market. As a member of the secretariat for the meeting, it was my role to brief them in advance as to what the forum expected, but despite that, some would come ill-prepared. The senior channel marketing decision-makers absolutely loved the Roman Colosseum atmosphere, where they could "pulverise" product managers, "smash" their strategic thinking, "machete" their P&L forecasts, and engage in a jolly good round of corporate blood-letting. It was sheer theatre, and often colleagues from other departments contacted me to see if they could be sneaked into the room as spectators to watch the performances. At the time, it was just the way things were done – it was the corporate culture – but looking back at it now, I do feel for the product managers who meandered mournfully out of the conference room with their tails between their legs and their plans in tatters.

8.4   Exercise: Disconnect

The internet is a powerful tool, but it is also a huge source of distraction and interruption. We can end up sitting on it for hours, bouncing around sites and media platforms, and before we know it, half a day has disappeared. We heard earlier how, in one study, 47 per cent of the time, subjects were mind wandering. This happens even more when we are on the internet and we can enter a sort of semi-somnambulant state.

Therefore, this weekend, try disconnecting entirely from the internet. If you can't manage the whole weekend, then at least try one day – no internet, no video streaming, nothing on your laptop, smartphone or television. However, it is vital that you plan what you will be doing. Consider whether you want to spend the time in the garden, go for a nature walk, paint on a canvas, read, write poetry or a short story, or play board games. Whatever it is, plan it in advance and make a clear intention when, where and what time you will do it. If you don't plan what you will do, you will feel the pangs of losing the internet and, most likely, be tempted back by the attention merchants.

8.5 Key points

Some of the critical points we covered in this chapter were as follows:

- Fortunately, most of the distractions in life can be constrained. This is a hopeful position to start from. It is within our ability to show restraint in matters to do with: email, phone alerts, meetings, social media, news websites, and messaging applications.
- When you are engaged in cognitively demanding work (or deep work), you want to avoid distractions at all costs.
- When you are doing cognitively demanding work and you remove distractions, you can maintain your energy levels for much longer, as you are not spending time jumping around from one thing to the next, with cortisol and adrenaline firing off.
- Even when you are operating in the shallows, carefully managing notifications, your smartphone, email and meetings will help boost your productivity and mental well-being.
- Try disconnecting from the internet for the weekend, but plan in advance what you will do with the free time; otherwise, you will be lured back to browsing the web.

Endnotes

1. "Email is not free", https://hbr.org/2013/04/email-is-not-free.
2. William J. Becker, Liuba Belkin and Sarah Tuskey, "Killing me softly: Electronic communications monitoring and employee and spouse well-being", *Academy of Management*, 9 July 2018.

Chapter 9
BEING SELECTIVE

Had I known how listening is superior to speaking,
I would not have wasted my life preaching

– Farid al-Din Attar.

9.1 Stalling

In order to actively initiate a response to being distracted, we need to overcome our own inertia, which keeps us from doing things we might consider difficult or we are unsure about. If you are going to undergo a transformation, minimise distraction in your life and find your purpose, this is necessary but hard – it's not easy. One thing that you will need to overcome is your in-built mechanism to stall, to delay, to procrastinate. Everyone procrastinates according to Tim Pychyl, author of *Solving the Procrastination Puzzle* (2010), and 20 per cent of people procrastinate chronically.[1]

In his two decades of research on the topic of procrastination, he found that the more unattractive a task or project is to you, the more likely you are to stall.

He found are were six main elements that make procrastination more likely. These are related to what extent the task at hand is one of the following: boring frustrating, difficult, unstructured or ambiguous, lacking in personal meaning and/or lacking in intrinsic rewards. The more of these elements a task contains, the more unpleasant it seems to us, and so we are likely to stall and avoid doing it.

Pychyl notes that: "Sometimes procrastination is just a symptom that your life just doesn't match what you're interested in and ... maybe you should do something else." I have definitely had this feeling many times in my career, and in truth, until I found my outside passions – writing and teaching – to balance against what paid the bills – my corporate career – I always felt out of balance, not quite whole. It wasn't until I was able to settle my energy across these three aspects of my life that I was able to overcome (most of the time) my inclination to procrastinate.

That doesn't mean this is what you should do. Rather, if you find yourself procrastinating at work, or at home, consider what other interests you can introduce into your life that will fulfil your purpose. That way, you won't have time to procrastinate as you will see time as a precious commodity not to be wasted.

In the meantime, if you find yourself procrastinating, come up with some ideas about how to overcome your tendency to stall and delay. Here are a few suggestions. If the task is:

- Boring: Introduce some relish and enjoyment into it. If you need to go through an archive of spreadsheets to understand the cost structure of a balance sheet, or you need to read the first draft of a tedious piece of legislation, or you need to complete a tiresome application form, visit a place you enjoy, such as a local coffee shop. Buy a coffee that stimulates you in a positive manner, and work through it.
- Frustrating: I often switch on a countdown timer for 30 or 45 minutes and then pile-drive through the task. When the counter hits zero, I will leave the task, go off for a while and do something I enjoy, such as listen to an audiobook, read a novel, or go for a quick walk whilst reflecting. I then return to the task, set a new countdown timer and then steamroll through it once more.
- Difficult: Every one of us has a time of day when we are at our peak. For some, this might be early morning; others, late morning; for others, in the late afternoon. You know when your body naturally is most energised. Tackle the difficult task when you can apply the most energy to it.
- Unstructured or ambiguous: Anyone who has worked in an advisory capacity will tell you that every task they have been asked to address by a client starts in the same way. The client knows there is a problem, but they just can't put their finger on it. Or they can put their finger on it, but just don't know why the problem exists. If you have a task such as this, then step back and deconstruct it into micro-tasks.

Ensure you maintain the causal links between tasks, not losing sight of how they remain connected to the whole. Then set yourself a plan to tackle one micro-task at a time. As a novelist, I don't write the novel in one sitting, but tackle it one chapter at a time, and often within each chapter, each sequence by each sequence, and within each sequence, each event by each event, and within each event, each beat by each beat. It's much more manageable that way, and you always feel a sense of momentum and progress.

- Lacking in personal meaning: I have had this so many times in my career that I've lost count. Why am I doing this? What is the point of it? This has nothing to do with me, and so on. When this happens, and it still does, I think about something that is meaningful to me, such as spending time with the family, reading, or cycling, and I tell myself if I can get through this drudgery of a task, then I will have more time to do the other thing, which has more meaning to me. This usually spurs me into action.
- Lacking in intrinsic rewards: In other words, there is nothing in this task that is internally rewarding to you. You don't feel proud, or more whole, or enriched by the experience of doing it. I know people who set aside a small monetary treat for themselves when they finish a task. Your treat will depend on your personal preferences, but it should be something that you rarely treat yourself with, not something you consume or do every day. The treat does not have to be about consumption.

For example, if you have a pet, then you may treat yourself with more time to play with the pet.

9.2 How to say "no"

Avoiding stalling or procrastinating, as we have just read, is about spurring yourself on to undertake a task that is boring, frustrating, difficult, unstructured or ambiguous, lacking in personal meaning and/or lacking in intrinsic rewards. This advice was given on the basis that we have no choice in the matter. Due to the circumstances we find ourselves in, we have to do the task. However, the opposite of this is also possible. In other words, when you have the option to say "no" to a task someone is trying to get you to do.

The late Peter Drucker, a management thinker, believed that "people are effective because they say no". It's important to be clear about this because if we take on a piece of work we are not sure about, it means we will not be able to do something else that may be more in line with our role at work or purpose in life. If you are not clear about your role and purpose, you can easily fall into the trap of saying yes, taking something on, and becoming stuck in the quagmire of purposeless activity, spiralling into a loss of certainty.

This approach might be less applicable to you if you are relatively junior in a large corporate where you are handed down tasks, but it is definitely advice we can all apply in our personal lives, and as we gain influence wherever we work, we can also bring this thinking to bear.

However, it's important to learn to say no with sophistication and delicacy. This starts by separating the person from the task. You are not saying no to the person. You are saying no to the task they are giving you. In the same manner, many faith-based teachings advise that you may dislike the actions of a person, but try not to dislike them, because deep down, they are the same as you, and you need to search for this common connection.

I have had times when I said no to a colleague or boss, and the immediate reaction was frosty, but this frustration soon melted away when we took on other work that was a lot more meaningful and in line with our goals as an organisation. If we had taken on the other task, which I did not believe was in line with our purpose, then we would not have had the capacity to deliver the work that was more in keeping with our goals. What my pushback has also shown me is that other people become more mindful of not wasting my time because they know what response they are going to receive. As a result, they work harder to set out the merits of what they bring to me because they know if it's in line with our goals and purpose, then I will be 100 per cent behind it and the deliverables they receive will be of the highest quality available.

Here are a couple of techniques you can use to say no, without actually mentioning the word "no":

1. "Currently I am totally occupied on Project X, but once this is complete in 10 weeks' time, I would be happy

to get together to talk about your requirements." If the task is urgent, they will find someone else to do it.
2. "I will need to check my availability on my calendar and can then drop you a note with some options." This provides you with more time to think through how you will say no.
3. "I can take a look at this, but what task do you want me to deprioritise?" This is a useful response to someone more senior than you.
4. "I am maxed out at this time and would not be able to deliver a high-quality piece of work should I take this on." This usually sends the one asking to another door, as no one wants to compromise on quality.
5. "I am totally booked up at the moment, but you might want to try 'X' person." If they need the task done, they will happily find another resource who can do it, and will be grateful to you for the referral. I have used this to refer business to others on numerous occasions. The person asking went away happy and the person taking on the work was grateful for the referral.

However you say no, do not leave any ambiguity over it. Be clear you are passing on the opportunity. This is a lot more professional than leaving someone thinking you might say yes and trying to make it work. If the task is important to them, they will find another resource. If you stall from saying no, then it only becomes harder later on, and the other person will most likely hold a grudge against you for it.

9.3 Rule of 9

Despite learning to say no with a degree of sophistication, an additional criterion you can apply to decisions about where to spend your precious time is a technique called the Rule of 9. It works like this: if you are utterly convinced, then do it; otherwise, ignore it. Let's take an example we can all relate to. Open your wardrobe, look at your clothes and ask yourself: "Am I ever going to wear this?"

If you are like most people, you have clothes in your wardrobe you have not worn for six months or even one year. Despite asking the question, you'll still keep the clothes. However, asking "Am I in love with this?" will allow you to eliminate the clutter and create space for something better. This can also be applied to the choices we make in life. I have a "maybe" area within my wardrobe. All the clothes I am uncertain about wearing, I shuffle to the right side of the cupboard and place a separator between them and the clothes I am using. I then take note of whether or not I have worn those clothes for six months. If I haven't, I give them away to charity. This rule applies to items like shirts, trousers, and sweaters.

You can apply the Rule of 9 to any decision. As you ponder over what to do, give the option a score between 0 and 10. If it is less than 9, simply ignore it. This allows you to avoid getting caught in the 6s and 7s – things you really don't want to be doing. What this will mean is that on occasion you may turn something down that was really good. That happens in life, but at least you made the choice and it wasn't forced upon you.

BEING SELECTIVE

Staying firm to the Rule of 9 can be tricky, particularly when opportunities start to present themselves. Maybe you get a call from a recruitment consultant about a role you weren't expecting. What should you do? It seems like an easy choice to make to apply for it, but does it really match your career aspirations and where you currently are in life?

I've had a number of occasions when I was approached for a more senior role, offering additional money, benefits and responsibility, but it didn't meet my Rule of 9, much to the surprise of the executive recruiter. I turned these more lucrative opportunities down, as I assessed them using the Rule of 9 in the following manner:

- I wrote out on a piece of paper the opportunity and how it was different to my existing role.
- I set three basic criteria the role should achieve: Is this interesting work? Does the company have a culture of meritocracy? What positive impact will the role have on stakeholders?
- I set three advanced criteria the role should achieve: Is this going to be an intellectually challenging environment where I can create new knowledge? Is the role going to allow me to continue my outside passions of writing and teaching? Is the role going to enable me to spend the requisite amount of time I want to with my family? More often than not, the last two on this list were not achievable, as the executive roles were all-consuming, involving global travel and long periods of time away from the family. For me, it

was not worth it – it didn't meet my Rule of 9 – so I politely turned the position down.

9.4 Passion at work is rare

Being selective about what assignments you take can be difficult when financial incentives and status are being dangled to tempt you to follow your dreams. The grass always seems greener on the other side, until you get there. Alongside promises of a better career on the other side of the hiring process, we are routinely encouraged to reach for the stars, pursue our dreams and follow our passions. These are the beloved mantras of many a motivational speaker and self-help guru. However, as career advice, especially for the young, it's paralysing.

Here's why. In one Canadian study, when university students were asked whether they were passionate about something, more than 84 per cent confirmed they were.[2] When asked what they were passionate about, the responses were: dance, hockey, skiing, reading, and swimming. Each country has slight variations, so rather than hockey, it might be football. However, what is evident is that none of these passions, for 99.9 per cent of students, will become a career.

So why do experienced executives peddle this advice to students and young workers? Unfortunately, conventional wisdom, due to self-help books on the topic, makes the case for following your passions. Equally, figures such as Steve Jobs spoke fluently about pursuing your dreams. Yet, Jobs' own life shows that in the years before he started Apple computers, he wasn't passionate about technology. He was passionate about yoga, meditation and Eastern mysticism. He only got involved in making and selling computers so that he could make a quick buck and finance his next trip back to India. When it unexpectedly took off, he stayed around, realised he was really good at it, and because he was really good at it, became passionate about it. Becoming really good came first; passion came second.

It's worth considering the difference between a job, a career, and a calling, as defined by Yale professor Amy Wrzesniewski.[3] A job, according Wrzesniewski, is a way to pay the bills, a career is a path toward increasingly better work, and a calling is work that's an important part of your life and a vital part of your identity. For example, my calling is being a storyteller. Outside of my job and career, I pursue this calling by writing historical fiction. However, I know it won't pay the bills. Perhaps at some point in the future, but not today.

Instead of shooting for the stars and ending up in the wrong constellation, take things in stages, because at the start of a career, you really don't know what you are going to love doing. Equally, most entry-level roles are not that interesting and you'll find your passion soon sizzling out. Better to work hard at the job you have and become as good as you can by forcing yourself through it, allowing your skills and craft to develop. Some writers refer to the rare and valuable skills we develop as career capital.[4] Whatever label you choose, becoming really good will mean people start to take notice of your efforts. Soon enough, your next job, more interesting work, and a career will be knocking at the door.

If you can approach work like a craftsman, your focus will be on what you can offer the world, as opposed to what the world can offer you. Becoming a craftsman enables you to sharpen skills that get you ahead. A craftsman does not become anxious about identifying the perfect job; they get on with the job at hand and become really good at it because they realise they have to earn it.

As the American satirist and novelist Mark Twain said: "The two most important days in your life are the day you are born and the day you find out why." Finding your passion is about what defines you, and makes you who you are. It's not what pays the bills. My advice: don't give up the day job whilst pursuing your passion.

9.5 Exercise: Becoming present

Before we close out ACT III, I'd like you to take a moment and do the following exercise.

1. Take a deep breath and become present in the moment. What is most important for you to do right now? Don't think about the future, later today, tomorrow, or next week. Ground yourself in the moment. If there are random thoughts entering your mind about other things, take a pen and paper and write them down. Then return your attention back to here and now.
2. The more you can stop thinking about the future, the easier it will become to focus on the present.

9.6 Key points

Some of the critical points we covered in this chapter were as follows:

- We procrastinate when a task is: boring frustrating, difficult, unstructured or ambiguous, lacking in personal meaning and/or lacking in intrinsic rewards.
- To overcome procrastination, come up with ideas about how to overcome your tendency to stall and delay.
- Learn to say no with sophistication and delicacy. This starts by separating the person from the task.
- However you say no, do not leave any ambiguity over it. Be clear you are passing on the opportunity. This is a lot more professional than leaving someone thinking you might say yes and trying to make it work.
- Apply the Rule of 9, which says that if you are utterly convinced about a matter, then do it; otherwise, ignore it.
- A job pays the bills, a career is a path toward increasingly better work, and a calling is work that's an important part of your life and a vital part of your identity, but it doesn't pay the bills (in most cases).
- Approach work like a craftsman, sharpen your skills, get on with the job at hand and become really good at it, and when you do, you will become passionate about it.

Endnotes

1. Timothy A. Pychyl, *Solving the Procrastination Puzzle*, 2010.
2. Vallerand, Blanchard, Mageau et al., "On Obsessive and Harmonious Passion", *Journal of Personality and Social Psychology 85*, no. 4, 2003, pp. 756-67.
3. Wrzesniewski, McCauley, Rozin et al., "Jobs, Careers and Callings: People's Relations to their Work", *Journal of Research in Personality 31*, 1997, pp. 21-33.
4. Cal Newport, *So Good They Can't Ignore You*, 2012.

ACT IV

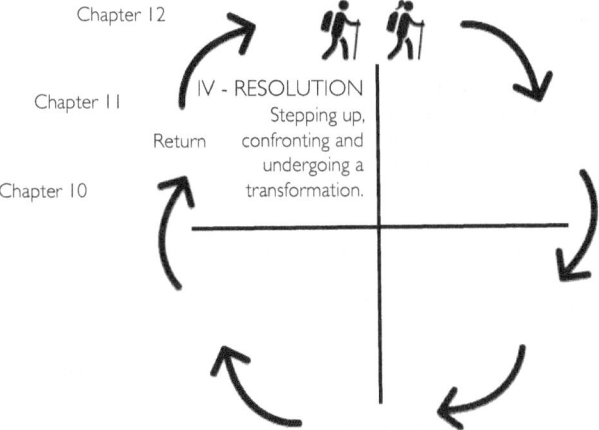

Chapter 12

Chapter 11

Chapter 10

Return

IV - RESOLUTION
Stepping up, confronting and undergoing a transformation.

Chapter 10
ATTENTION ENDURANCE

> Alone we can do so little; together we can do so much
>
> – Helen Keller.

10.1 Making your work harder

As we move into Act IV of our journey, we now start to address how you can transform your work and personal life. As we do, let's take a moment to think about why our mind wanders. As we mentioned earlier, our mind wanders about 47 per cent of the time. Our mind will wander more when:

- We feel worried or weary.
- We operate in a messy environment.
- We are dealing with a number of personal concerns.
- We question whether our tasks are meaningful.

- We are not fully using our attention.

One way to reduce the amount of time we aimlessly mind wander is to deliberately make our tasks more complex and take on more complex ones. In his book *Flow*, Mihaly Csikszentmihalyi suggests we are most likely to enter into a flow state when the challenge of completing a task is roughly equal to our ability to do so, and we become totally immersed in the task.[1] When our skills greatly exceed the demands of a task, such as doing data input for half a day, we end up feeling bored. When the demands of a task exceed our skills, such as having to give a presentation we are not prepared for, we feel anxious. However, when the demands of a task are roughly equal to our ability to do that task – reading a pleasurable book, playing a sport we have a high level of proficiency at, strumming an instrument, painting on a canvas – we are a lot more likely to be fully engaged in what we are doing.

One of the tell-tale signs I encountered that encouraged me to move jobs in the past was when I found my mind often wandering off the tasks I was doing, as the tasks were not difficult enough to consume my attention. In other words, I could do a lot more, and was being underutilised. I have also had the opposite experience, when I felt anxious at work because I realised that my skills at the time were not a good match for the tasks I had to do as part of the job. In both cases, I sought out new opportunities where I had a better match with the skills I had to offer and the difficulty of the tasks.

10.2   Intellect can be cultivated

When we cognitively stretch our minds and our tasks are complex enough to consume our attentional space, we have greater scope to grow our intelligence. Alfred Binet, the inventor of the IQ test, believed that children's intelligence was changeable. We are often led to believe otherwise. Binet, a Frenchman working in Paris in the early 20th century, designed the IQ test to identify children who were not profiting from the Paris public schools, so that new educational programs could be designed to get them back on track. Without denying individual differences in children's intellects, he believed that education and practice could bring about fundamental changes in intelligence. Here is a quote from one of his major books, *Modern Ideas About Children*, in which he summarises his work with hundreds of children with learning difficulties:

> A few modern philosophers assert that an individual's intelligence is a fixed quantity, a quantity which cannot be increased. We must protest and react against this brutal pessimism … With practice, training, and above all, method, we manage to increase our attention, our memory, our judgment and literally to become more intelligent than we were before.

Binet is arguing against the belief our intelligence is fixed and is offering a hopeful message that, with practice, training, and method, we can increase our attention, our memory, our judgment and literally become more intelligent than we were before. Elsewhere, Gilbert Gottlieb, an eminent neuroscientist, says that not only do genes and the environment cooperate as we develop, but genes require input from the environment to work properly.

10.3 Prime time

Along with believing we can become more intelligent with the right method and the right mindset, we must all be mindful that our energy levels tend to fluctuate throughout the day. Some of us have high energy levels in the morning; others feel more energised in the evening. If we have a coffee, we feel a burst of energy, but then will fall low on energy when the effects of the caffeine wear off. We all tend to feel a crash in energy levels after a heavy lunch, as our stomach starts the difficult tasks of breaking all of the food down, and so requires any spare energy to be directed to the stomach area.

This high peak time period is referred to by different names. One such is Biological Prime Time (BPT), a phrase coined by Sam Carpenter in his book *Work the System*.[2] Managing our time, but also managing our energy levels throughout the day, ensures we avoid becoming distracted when we grow tired, and we are able to continue to focus on the tasks at hand.

I often keep a time log so I can check in on myself every hour to ensure I'm staying on tasks, not becoming distracted by the trivial, and not procrastinating and putting off essential work. This allows me to review at the end of the day how I have been spending my time. The great thing with an hourly time log is that you don't have to wait till the end of the day to hold yourself accountable. If you are veering off your desired path, you will be able to quickly rectify your position and get back on track.

One study of nearly 1,700 participants showed that keeping a food diary can double a person's weight loss.[3] The study found that the best predictors of weight loss were how frequently food diaries were kept and how many support sessions the participants attended. Those who kept daily food records lost twice as much weight as those who kept no records. The same effect can be seen when you keep a time log – you manage to reduce the level of distractions and increase your focus and attention.

10.4 Rituals

As a professional who is looking to minimise distraction, and find purpose and meaning, you can't afford to be haphazard in your habits. The Pulitzer Prize–winning biographer Robert Caro, as was revealed in a 2009 magazine profile, explained how every inch of his New York office was governed by rules.[4] He had rules about where he placed his books (research on his immediate subject was closest), how he stacked his notebooks (new interviews were stacked at the top), what he put on the wall (an outline of the book he was working on), and even what he wore to the office. Everything had a routine, so that he could bring his full attention to his writing.

"I trained myself to be organised," he explained as he pointed almost apologetically at his massive writer's map. "If you're fumbling around trying to remember what notebook has what quote, you can't be in the room with the people you're writing about." Even Caro's home was governed by a code he created to keep himself productive and sane. His apartment was filled with books, but there was none in the dining or living rooms. And he did not discuss his work subjects at home.

David Brooks summarises this reality more bluntly: "Great creative minds think like artists but work like accountants." Caro was not being bizarre. Rather, he knew that success in his work relied on his ability to think deeply, and one way of facilitating this was to remove all distractions from his working environment. You may not be writing a Pulitzer Prize–winning piece, but you will be working on creating value in your organisation and personal life, and why not give yourself the best possible opportunity to excel at it?

If I haven't planned in advance, every time I sit down to write the novel I'm working on, I have to remind myself: What was the last paragraph I wrote? Where did I leave the story? Whose point of view was I in? What's their true character? This can eat up a lot of time. I, like the majority of writers, also have a day job. Others have family commitments, which means the time set aside for writing must be golden and facilitate depth. As a result, I always plan the night before. For example, tomorrow, I'm writing the chapter from

Character A's point of view and she will be doing such and such. That way, when I sit down in the morning, it takes me about 15 minutes to start to hit a rich vein of writing, when I know I'm deep enough.

Just to be clear, when working on a novel, I have never just sat down and started writing. It used to take about 30 minutes to achieve a flow state; now, it's about 15 minutes. It's like when an athlete is preparing to run the 400 metres – they will be warming up before commencing the race. The warm-up I do as a writer can consist of any of the following: sipping a good cup of tea, staring out of the window, taking deep breaths to become present in the moment, stretching, doodling on a piece of paper, making a picture of the last scene I wrote, or writing some warm-up paragraphs in bullet points so that I can see the beats in the scene. What I never do is use anything electronic, other than the software I'm using for typing my story, because I know I'll be sucked into a digital black hole, and the time I had ring-fenced for my writing will be eroded. Now, you might be able to get into this deep flow state within five minutes, and that's great, but the point is that it will take time, and you must force yourself through the barren plain of silence before you arrive at a field of your mind's harvest.

Here are some things you might want to think about in terms of your working rituals:

- How long are you going to work and where? Location is important and you must spend some time preparing it so that you can perform your best work there.

- What method and rules will you deploy when you work? For example, will you set yourself a timer for a 30-minute burst of work, or will you write for a couple of pages, or will you ensure you do not browse the internet for the first hour, or will you turn off Wi-Fi from your laptop so you can focus on the task?
- What will you support yourself with? For example, a good cup of coffee or tea, or the right level of food, or a short exercise break, every 45 minutes.

Whenever I'm at my most productive, I'm usually in a routine where I don't need to think too hard about where I work, how I will work or what will support my work. I plan all this in advance. I can then use all my energy on my most creative tasks.

Between 2014 and 2019, I wrote five novels. Obviously, this is over and above the day job, teaching commitments, spending time with the family and overall avoiding feeling like I was too busy. Between September and April of every year, I would write one novel. My routine went something like this. I woke up at 5:30am, prayed, drank some green tea. Started to get ready for the day. By 6:45am, my laptop came on and I began to write. (I planned the night before what I was going to write, so this allowed my mind to mull it over whilst I slept.) I took a working breakfast around 7:30am, with tea. I finished at 8:30am, after which, I headed off to my day job. Normally, I would have written 1000 words during this period. In the evening, I did my planning but no writing. (I don't produce my best work late at night.) I started getting ready for bed by 9pm, so no smartphone after that. I got into bed before 9:30pm, read for about 20 minutes, and aimed to be asleep before 10pm. That way, I was sleeping between 7.5 and 8 hours per night. On the weekend, I used a few hours in the morning, again rising early, to review what I wrote during the week (approximately 5000 words) before I started to write afresh the following week.

When I'm writing a novel, I know that if I don't establish these rituals, my novel will drag out. It took me four years to write my first novel, 24 months to write my second, 18 months for the third, 12 months for the fourth and just over nine months for the fifth. I am just finishing the sixth novel and it has taken about seven months. Each time, I kept optimising and improving my processes to enable me to get deep more quickly and stay there for longer.

10.5   Key points

Some of the critical points we covered in this chapter were as follows:

- One way to reduce the amount of time we aimlessly mind wander is to deliberately make our tasks more complex and take on more complex ones.
- When we cognitively stretch our minds and our tasks are complex enough to consume our attentional space, we have greater scope to grow our intelligence.

- Managing our time, but also managing our energy levels throughout the day, ensures we avoid becoming distracted when we grow tired, and we are able to continue to focus on the tasks at hand.
- Success in work is down to your ability to think deeply, and one way of facilitating this is to remove all distractions from the working environment.
- You will be at your most productive when you are in a routine where you don't need to think too hard about where to work, how to work or what will support your work. Instead, you use your energy to dive deep into your work.

Endnotes

1. Mihaly Csikszentmihalyi, *Flow*, 1990.
2. Sam Carpenter, *Work the System*, 2008.
3. *Science Daily* https://www.sciencedaily.com/releases/2008/07/080708080738.htm.
4. "The Marathon Man", *Newsweek*, February 16, 2009.

Chapter 11
RECHARGING

> Every morning was a cheerful invitation to make my life of equal simplicity, and I may say innocence, with nature herself
>
> – Henry David Thoreau.

11.1 Sleeping for the job

A few more clicks on the mouse, a couple more swipes on the smartphone, I tell myself, and I'll get off to bed. But it doesn't happen. Instead, when I glance back at the time, I realise the promise of getting to sleep early has gone by the wayside. Tomorrow night, I console myself, I'll get to sleep early so I don't wake up feeling like a train wreck.

Since we've all done this ourselves and regretted it, the impact is not only personal but also organisational. In fact, there is a huge cost to the effectiveness of an organisation due to sleep deprivation.

According to Gallup, 40 per cent of Americans get less than the recommended seven to nine hours every night.[1] The Centers for Disease Control and Prevention have labelled this lack of sleep a "public health epidemic" because of the huge health and performance costs associated with not getting enough sleep.[2] In a study by Vicki Culpin, she and her team monitored the sleep behaviour of 1,000 professionals at all levels, and the impact of sleep on workplace performance.[3]

The team's findings suggested that lack of sleep can fundamentally hinder a manager's ability to perform at their peak and leads to other damaging physical and emotional side effects. "It is common for managers and colleagues to look at a lack of focus or motivation, irritability, and bad decision making as being caused by poor training, organizational politics or the work environment. The answer could be much simpler – a lack of sleep," according to Culpin.

In addition, there are also the physiological impacts on the individual, one primary issue being an erosion of one's immune system – a topic of much debate in the middle of a global pandemic. According to research undertaken by the Harvard Centre for Healthy Sleeping, interactions between sleep and the immune system have been well-documented.[4] They suggest that sleep deprivation may decrease the ability to resist infections, such as the common cold. In one study cited by Harvard, the researchers found that people who averaged less than seven hours of sleep a night were about three times more likely to develop cold symptoms when exposed to the cold-causing rhinovirus than study volunteers who got eight or more hours of sleep.[5]

The more sleep you get, up to the recommended seven to nine hours, the more energy you will have the next day. Sleep affects your mood, ability to focus, and how you tackle problems, learn, and remember. And lack of sleep negatively impacts your concentration, working memory, and mathematical reasoning abilities.

When you add a bad diet and little exercise into the mix, your energy levels and productivity can spiral out of control pretty quickly. You are also far more susceptible to falling prey to distractions around you, as you try to let dopamine hits in your brain give you the sense of being busy. This is something important to keep in mind when it comes to getting enough sleep. The key to getting enough sleep is going to bed at the right time.

When I found that lack of sleep was affecting my ability to perform at work, as well as write my novels, I created a night-time routine so that my alarm went off at 9pm and this meant that I needed to start getting ready to go to sleep. For me, this meant closing down all my electronic items, being in bed by 9:30pm, reading for 20 minutes and then falling asleep shortly after 10pm, so that I could wake up feeling really fresh. It gave a huge boost to my performance and creativity. You need to work out a bedtime routine that works for you and your personal circumstances. However you run it, you should be aiming to get seven to eight hours of uninterrupted sleep. I appreciate that if you have young children, of course, this is not always possible. I fondly remember my own children turning up beside my bed early on a Saturday morning and asking me to switch myself on. It was 6am.

If you want to help yourself become more effective, and your organisation achieve its goals, then rest your head on your pillow and start sleeping for the job.

11.2 Maintaining energy

When I start to become distracted, struggle to focus, and get sidetracked in the trivial, it's a sure sign that I am short of sleep. I often slip into coasting, not thinking about what I should be doing. Some of the other signs that indicate my energy levels are low are the following:

- Regular task switching and struggling to concentrate.
- Intentions falling away and becoming more haphazard.
- Completing tasks much more slowly, due to such things as having to re-read a paragraph more than normal.
- Gravitating towards trivial tasks, such as checking email and social feeds.

To overcome this, I have a set of activities I try to initiate by way of taking a break from the work I am doing. These involve: going for a walk, doing a high-intensity workout, or listening to an audiobook or podcast. Here are some other suggestions that you might also want to try:

- Taking a brisk walk. If it's in a green area, that's even better.
- Listening to or reading an enjoyable story.
- Chatting with some friends.
- Meditating or praying.
- Listening to some relaxing music.
- Serving others, whether they are family members or people in need.
- Spending time on a craft, such as woodwork, painting, or photography.

How often you need to take a break will vary on a number of factors, including what type of person you are – outgoing or more introverted. The research points to significant advantages acquired from taking regular breaks as well as a lunch break.[6] The benefits being:

- Improved productivity. Breaks can boost productivity as you can reset your focus and energy levels when you step away from work. A lunch break can also help you to avoid the afternoon energy slump, so long as you have not overeaten!
- Well-being. Taking a break away from work can help to reduce stress, especially if you can combine it with a healthy lunch and a walk.
- Creativity surge. Stepping away from work can bring a fresh perspective. If you are looking at the same thing the whole day, it can become difficult to make progress. A break stimulates more creative thinking.

- Healthier habits. Breaks can allow for more healthy eating habits, exercise, meditation and care for oneself.

If you can build in a 10- to 15-minute break every hour, or a 20- to 30-minute break every 90 minutes, then you are going to help yourself not become distracted. Our energy levels, much like REM sleep, operate in 90-minute intervals, and taking a break after this period aligns with our bodily rhythms.

Typically, my day job starts at 9am, and I tend to take a tea break at 10:30am, 90 minutes in, when I can feel the energy levels flagging a little. After the break, I then work for another 90 minutes, before another quick break, then have one shorter session, which takes me through to lunch around 1pm. I then repeat this for the afternoon, working in short bursts and taking regular breaks to recharge my energy levels.

11.3 Refuel mind and body

Along with ensuring you are getting sufficient sleep every night and are maintaining the right energy levels throughout the day, there are a couple of other things you can pay attention to that will help you become less distracted. These are related to what you eat, what you drink and how much exercise you do.

- Eat more unprocessed food: It takes longer for the body to digest unprocessed food. The body converts whatever we eat into glucose – a sugar our body and brain burn for energy. Unprocessed food takes longer to digest, as our body switches it to glucose at a much slower rate, providing us with a steady drip of energy throughout the day. Processed food gets converted into glucose quickly, but it does not provide us with as much energy over a longer period of time. Also when you eat, don't fill your stomach. Traditional societies and cultures suggested filling your stomach with a third for food, a third for water and a third for air. If we stuff ourselves silly, then we are left feeling sluggish, as our body struggles to digest the excessive food in the stomach.

- Caffeine and water: Caffeine prevents your brain from absorbing a chemical called adenosine, which normally tells your body it's tired. It takes about 8–14 hours after you have consumed caffeine for your body to metabolise it out of your system. When I consumed caffeine for productivity purposes, I drank it between 9:30 and 10:30am. This is when caffeine had the greatest impact on my energy levels and didn't disrupt my night-time sleep. Whilst travelling overseas on business trips, I've often drunk coffee mid-morning when I have a night-time flight, so that as the effect starts to wear off, I'm ready to sleep on the airplane. Or if I've taken an overnight flight and landed the next day and had to go into work, I've taken a coffee shortly after landing so that my body can last till early evening, when I head straight to bed and crash out for a long night's sleep. I would also suggest that you drink water first thing in the morning. I normally

drink two glasses of room-temperature water after I wake up. There are a number of studies on the benefits of drinking water. Some suggest that it fires up our metabolism in the morning. Another study found that people who drank water before meals lost weight because water partly fills the stomach. Water also helps us think more clearly and reduces the risk of certain diseases and ailments.
- Exercise: When we workout, especially with aerobic exercise, our brain releases a number of chemicals that allow us to fight stress. We also increase the blood flow to the brain, which is positive for our mental performance – we feel less tired and have more focus. When we exercise, our brain releases BDNF (brain-derived neurotrophic factor), a chemical that helps create new brain cells – a lot of this growth happens in the hippocampus, the part of your brain responsible for memory. Exercise can even boost mood and build cells in brain regions damaged by depression.

11.4 Key points

Some of the critical points we covered in this chapter were as follows:

- Lack of sleep can fundamentally hinder your ability to perform at your peak and lead to other damaging physical and emotional side effects.

- Sleep deprivation may decrease the ability to resist infections, such as the common cold. Studies showed that people who averaged less than seven hours of sleep a night were about three times more likely to develop cold symptoms than study volunteers who got eight or more hours of sleep when exposed to the cold-causing rhinovirus.
- To maintain your energy levels, have a set of activities that you can do to take a break from work, such as going for a walk, doing a high-intensity workout, or listening to an audiobook or podcast.
- Eat more unprocessed food, as it takes longer for the body to digest. Caffeine, when taken at the right time, can boost your productivity. Water helps you think clearly and fights off disease. Exercise boosts our mood and helps our brains develop.

Endnotes

1. "In U.S., 40% Get Less Than Recommended Amount of Sleep", Gallup, https://news.gallup.com/poll/166553/less-recommended-amount-sleep.aspx#:~:text=PRINCETON%2C%20NJ%20%2D%2D%20Fifty%2Dnine,much%20more%20in%20the%201940s.
2. "CDC Declares Sleep Disorders a Public Health Epidemic", https://www.sleepdr.com/the-sleep-blog/cdc-declares-sleep-disorders-a-public-health-epidemic/.
3. "The Wake-up Call; The importance of sleep in organizational life", HULT Ashridge, https://www.hult.edu/en/executive-education/insights/the-wakeup-call/.
4. "Sleep and health", Harvard, http://healthysleep.med.harvard.edu/need-sleep/whats-in-it-for-you/health.
5. S. Cohen et al., "Sleep Habits and Susceptibility to the Common Cold", *Arch of Intern Med.*, 169 (1), 12 Jan 2009, pp. 62-67.
6. "New Study Shows Correlation Between Employee Engagement And The Long-Lost Lunch Break", Forbes https://www.forbes.com/sites/alankohll/2018/05/29/new-study-shows-correlation-between-employee-engagement-and-the-long-lost-lunch-break/?sh=78f209eb4efc.

Chapter 12
TRANSFORMING

> The only person you are destined to become is the person you decide to be
>
> – Ralph Waldo Emerson.

12.1 Learning a craft

When you ensure you are sleeping enough, maintain your energy levels throughout the day and are also eating and drinking the right sort of thing, you will have set yourself up for success. The question that remains is what you will do with your newfound time, preferably moments and periods in the day when you are not distracted by the trivial and the mundane.

One of the avenues you may wish to explore is to consider a craft, preferably an activity you can do with your hands. Gary Rogowski is a furniture maker based in Portland, Oregon (US), who published a book titled *Handmade* (2017). He writes:

> People have the need to put their hands-on tools and to make things ... we need this in order to feel whole ... Long ago we learned to think by using our hands, not the other way around. Many people experience the world largely through a screen now. We live in a world that is working to eliminate touch as one of our senses, to minimize the use of our hands to do things except poke at a screen.[1]

When we immerse ourselves in a craft, and leave the digital world, it makes us more human, and we obtain a deeper satisfaction from it. Rogowski advises: "Leave good evidence of yourself ... do good work." That is, use skills to produce valuable things in the physical world.

The British Journal of Occupational Therapy found that the craft of knitting had a positive impact on personal and social well-being.[2] The research was undertaken with 3,545 knitters worldwide. The study aimed to identify the benefits of knitting for individuals' personal and social well-being as a prerequisite to investigating its therapeutic use. Respondents came from a virtual community of knitters. The majority were female white adults and frequent knitters, who commonly reported knitting for relaxation, stress relief and creativity. The results showed a significant relationship between knitting frequency and feeling calm and happy. More frequent knitters also reported higher cognitive functioning. Knitting in a group impacted significantly on perceived happiness, and improved social contact and communication with others. The researchers concluded that knitting has significant psychological and social benefits, which can contribute to well-being and quality of life. As a skilled and creative occupation, it has therapeutic potential – an area requiring further research.

Whether you take up knitting or another craft, the learning here is that performing a craft improves well-being. The craft you pursue may be performed by yourself, but if you can add a social dimension to it, studies show that this brings additional therapeutic benefits. In one Scandinavian study, the researchers discovered that when performing a craft, handling physical material can help regulate mental states through providing a means to reach flow states.[3] Carrying out these tasks also enables us to fail safely and regulate our emotions, and facilitates social activity for many individuals who are at risk of social isolation.

A popular culture example of the social well-being phenomenon of crafts and leisure can be found in the resurgence of popular board games. David Sax in his 2016 book, *The Revenge of Analog*, reports that on weekends, the Snakes & Lattes café in Toronto seats 120 customers, with the line to enter the café leaking out onto the street.[4] The wait for a table can be up to three hours. Snakes & Lattes is a board-game café: you enter with a group of friends, are assigned a table, and then can select any game you want to play from the café's extensive library.

Playing a board game live with other people means you expose your emotions and feelings to others, as they do you. You can scrutinise their body language, and work out whether they are bluffing or genuinely have the upper hand.

These are complex social matches, which push our cognitive abilities to their limits. According to game theorist Scott Nicholson, there are two important aspects of engaging in a social leisure activity:

- The craft or leisure activity must involve spending time with others.
- The activity must have some type of structure or rules for the social interaction, as well as insider rituals and a shared goal.[5]

Nicholson says there are five elements that are important for the development of the game experience archetypes:

- The knowledge that the players bring to the game (Knowledge).
- The social interactions between players due to the game (Social).
- The engagement between players and the narrative of the game (Narrative).
- The decisions required by the player in changing the game state (Strategy).
- The actions required by the player in changing the game state (Action).

These five concepts – Social, Narrative, Actions, Knowledge, and Strategy (SNAKS) – are the underlying concepts for the game experience archetypes.

TRANSFORMING

Here are some practical suggestions about how you can take up a craft or use your leisure time in a manner that is more in line with your purpose in life:

- Repair or construct: Find a non-digital activity that you can do with your hands. Ideally, this should involve learning to repair or construct something. Don't overcomplicate it to begin with, but start with simple activities where you can follow a step-by-step process. For example: repairing the tyre on your bike, building a small coffee table for your living room, learning the basics of a new instrument. Whatever indoor or outdoor activity takes your fancy, probably one of the easiest ways to learn is to use YouTube. There are thousands of genuine enthusiasts who have posted simple teaching steps. Once you have the basics of something, go deeper, or rotate to another activity you might want to try. Set yourself some monthly goals, and within half a year, you may have added new skills you never expected you could have mastered.
- Protect your leisure time: Perhaps the best way to do this is to be clear on what you will do in your spare time. Are you going to learn a new craft or skill? It also means making a conscious decision as to how much time you will allocate to distractive pursuits, such as internet browsing, social media, entertainment sites and so on. There is no reason to go completely cold turkey on these distractions, as

you won't end up feeling good about it, and there is no point punishing yourself. It is better to take small incremental steps and build sustainable new practices than trying to take a huge leap in one go and end up floundering over the abyss. Therefore, schedule time to indulge yourself with these trivial distractions. Set a timer and then come out when the time finishes. In most cases, you will find that you don't need to spend more than 30 minutes a week on social-media sites. This absolutely terrifies the social-media companies, whose entire business model is based on keeping you glued to the screen, as their new and novel content fires off dopamine in your brain.

- Plan your time: Set yourself some tangible goals about what you will do in the non-digital time you have carved out for yourself. The goal should be underpinned by some practices that help you work towards the goal. For example, your goal might be to start playing tennis again. The practices you put in place might be: getting fit by doing a 20-minute, high-intensity workout three times a week, getting your tennis rackets restrung, eating well, and playing tennis competitively three to five times a week. To focus yourself towards your goal, you might want to enter a tennis tournament for your age group that is due to take place in three months' time. Being specific is really important here. You could have just said "play more tennis" but the goal would be too vague. Having a tournament to prepare for will really help sharpen your attention as well as fill the

time, which you might otherwise have been using to become distracted by the trivial.
- Sign-up: One of the best ways to avoid becoming distracted by the trivial is to join a group of other people who are engaged in some sort of activity. This could be a local sports league, a hobby group, a local charity, a rambling group, a fantasy gaming league, a school parents group, an environmental clean-up committee, or a religious society. We are all different and will have divergent interests – choose one thing and get started. It doesn't mean you are committing yourself for the next few years on this. You are merely reaching out to make real social connections with real people. See where it takes you.

If you remove low-value digital distractions from your life before replacing the void with something more meaningful, the experience may be rather unpleasant. As a result, first renovate your life, and decide what you will do in your spare time. When you fill the void with meaningful pursuits, you will find the digital distractions you used to be consumed by suddenly appear trivial and frivolous and will melt away from your horizons.

12.2 Set boundaries

Clayton Christensen, the Harvard business professor and author of *The Innovator's Dilemma*, was working for a management consulting firm earlier in his career. One of the partners came to him and told him he needed to come in on Saturday to help work on a project. Christensen responded: "Oh, I am so sorry. I have made the commitment that every Saturday is a day to be with my wife and children." The partner was not pleased and returned later to announce: "Clay, fine. I have talked with everyone on the team and they said they will come in on Sunday instead. So I will expect you to be there." Christensen sighed and said: "I appreciate you trying to do that. But Sunday will not work. I have given Sunday to God and so I won't be able to come in." I can just imagine the partner with a face like thunder, but Christensen was not sacked. His decision was not a popular one, but in the long-term, I suspect he was respected for holding his ground.

When we set boundaries, there will be some opportunities we miss, but if we don't set them, we can become spread too thin and will be distracted, which does not help us fulfil our purpose and meaning in life. Partly this ability to refuse non-vital tasks is also down to how much self-control we have. Scientists who have examined people who possess remarkable self-control realise that these individuals are not so different from those who are struggling. Rather, what they are better at is organising their lives in a way that means they do not have to exert incredible powers of self-control. In other words, they spend less time in tempting situations.[6] As they avoid enticing settings, they need to draw-down less on their self-restraint.[7]

This idea makes sense when you understand what happens when a habit is formed in the brain. A habit that has been encoded in the mind is ready to be used whenever the relevant situation arises. I remember being in gatherings with my father in the 1970s. He wasn't a smoker. Yet, when he sat with a certain group of friends who were and they offered him a cigarette, he would always accept, much to the consternation of my mother. It was an old habit with this group of friends, which had been coded in the 1960s. So even though he never smoked himself, with this particular social circle, he did take the odd puff. Once the neural pathways have been carved into the brain, it's nearly impossible to remove them entirely. And so the best strategy is to avoid the situation in the first place.

12.3 Inherent beliefs

Setting boundaries, showing self-restraint and avoiding tempting situations are all behaviours that will help us avoid trivial distractions. Another aspect that we need to consider is the inherent beliefs or, as Carol Dweck, professor of psychology, says, our mindset.[8] She relates the story of some children who were asked to solve a set of puzzles. Some of the children struggled, and others found it too difficult, but there was one ten-year-old boy who rubbed his hands together, smacked his lips, and cried out, "I love a challenge!" Another, sweating away on these puzzles, looked up with a pleased expression and said with authority, "You know, I was hoping this would be informative!"

Dweck says that what these children inherently knew was that human qualities, such as intellectual skills, can be cultivated. They were tackling the problem because it was going to make them smarter, and when they failed, they didn't regard it as a failure, but simply as a process of learning. Dweck's work points us to two types of inherent beliefs, or mindsets: one is a fixed mindset and the other is a growth mindset.

> Believing that your qualities are carved in stone—the fixed mindset—creates an urgency to prove yourself over and over. If you have only a certain amount of intelligence, a certain personality, and a certain moral character—well, then you'd better prove that you have a healthy dose of them ...
> There's another mindset in which these traits are not simply a hand you're dealt and have to live with. This growth mindset is based on the belief that your basic qualities are things you can cultivate through your efforts, your strategies, and help from others.
> The passion for stretching yourself and sticking to it, even (or especially) when it's not going well, is the hallmark of the growth mindset. This is the mindset that allows people to thrive during some of the most challenging times in their lives.

In the world of the fixed mindset, it's all about proving you are smart and talented. In the growth mindset, it is about stretching yourself to learn something new. In the fixed mindset, effort is a bad thing – things should just come naturally. In the growth mindset, effort is what makes you smart and talented.

Benjamin Bloom was a prominent educational researcher. One of his studies observed 120 outstanding achievers. Amongst the cohort were concert pianists, sculptors, Olympic swimmers, world-class tennis players, mathematicians, and research neurologists. He found that most were not that remarkable as children and didn't show clear talent before their training began in earnest. Even by early adolescence, you usually couldn't predict their future accomplishment from the ability they showed at the time. It was only their continued motivation and commitment, along with their support network, that took them to the top of their profession. Bloom observed:

> After forty years of intensive research on school learning in the United States as well as abroad, my major conclusion is: What any person in the world can learn, almost all persons can learn, if provided with the appropriate prior and current conditions of learning.[9]

The above comment did not include the 2 to 3 per cent of children who had severe learning impairments, nor the top 1 to 2 per cent of children at the other end of the spectrum. He was referring to everybody else.

In the world of business, Malcolm Gladwell refers to this fixed mindset as the "talent mindset" and says this is the new orthodoxy of American management. It led to disasters like the collapse of Enron. The firm was a huge believer in recruiting top talent with major qualifications, paying them huge sums of money, but by relying completely on talent, Enron fatally created a culture in which talent was worshipped. As a result, employees always behaved like they knew exactly what was going on, since they were huge talents, and were not able to spot or correct their shortcomings.

In *Good to Great*, Jim Collins addressed the factors that allowed some companies to thrive. There were many, but one was down to the type of leader in place. Great companies were not led by a know-it-all, self-proclaimed talent. Rather, they were led by rather humble individuals, who were curious, asked lots of questions, and confronted the most brutal answers and their own failures whilst they maintained the belief that, in the end, they would succeed. These were leaders who had a growth mindset. They were perennial learners who believed in human development and constantly trying to improve. As a result, they were always looking at what skills the company would need in the future and based their decisions on facts, rather than relying on talent to miraculously make it right.

12.4 Defiance is possible

With the development of a growth mindset and a set of inherent beliefs that steers us away from distraction, we will find ourselves in a much stronger position to resist trivial digital frivolity. Tim Wu, a law professor, highlights the attention economy, which, he says, "describes the business sector that makes money gathering consumers' attention and then repackaging and selling it to advertisers".[10]

He says that, driven by the needs of a small cadre of technology investors, companies like Facebook innovated in the domain of attention engineering, learning to exploit psychological vulnerabilities within all of us, scientifically and surgically giving us a dopamine shot to keep us glued to our screens. This is the classic profitable use case of the attention economy. The more we stay bonded to our screens, the more money the attention merchants make from advertisers.

As the Silicon Valley inventor and pioneer of virtual reality Jaron Lanier so aptly describes:

> We must learn to see the full picture, and not just the treats before our eyes. Our trendy gadgets, smartphones and tablets, have given us new access to the world. We regularly communicate with people we would never even have been aware of before the networked age.
>
> We can find information about almost anything at any time. But we have learned how much our gadgets and our idealistically motivated digital networks are being used to spy on us by ultra-powerful, remote organizations. We are being dissected more than we dissect.[11]

How, then, can we defy this tidal wave, when there is so much stacked against us and the lure of being distracted is at every turn, every room in our homes, every moment of downtime? To start with, we need to ask ourselves a simple question: what job does Facebook, or similar services, do for me? In other words, what would be the things that we would genuinely miss if we were to stop using Facebook or an equivalent? You may find the list is far shorter than you expected.

Now consider the following scenario – one championed by Jaron Lanier in his book *Who Owns the Future* (2014) – what if Facebook charged by the minute for using its service? Then ask yourself how much time you would actually need to spend on Facebook every week. It's quite likely to shrink down to 20–30 minutes for the whole week, whereas the average user currently spends anywhere from 300–350 minutes per week. In addition, they will often be users of other social-media services, such as Twitter and Instagram, plus popular news feeds.

In reality, Facebook is not charging us by the minute, so let's then imagine that the charge is not a financial one, but it is a psychological one, or if you are more spiritually inclined, a metaphysical one, draining your very mind and soul, making you into something and someone you are not. What non-financial cost are you willing to pay?

If you need to use Facebook, consider how it brings value to your purpose in life and then limit your use to that only. Like any bad habit, it creeps up on you, and before you know it, you are consumed by it.

Here are some practical suggestions about how you can show defiance against the attention merchants:

- Make social media invisible on your smartphone: I have all of my social-media apps on the fifth page of my smartphone. The possibility of me checking it remains remote. I tend to use my laptop to check in once or twice a week. If I'm at an event or there is an urgent need to respond, then I'll use my smartphone. If you remove the signal, the social-media app, from your field of view, then you won't end up going to it every time you have downtime. I am not suggesting you abandon the service, only use it to add some value to your life. For me as an author, its value is that it allows me to keep in touch with readers, make announcements about books, and so on. That is the only reason I use social media. Also imagine for a moment that a fast-forward, time-lapse video of your entire life was playing whilst you rested on your deathbed, surrounded by your family and friends. What would it show? Would it depict you spending your life watching TV, browsing social media, scrolling on your smartphone? I am sure you would not want this, and nor would I. It's a thought experiment today, but in the near future, such a capability may exist as humans become more receptive to having technology fused into their own minds and bodies.
- Be surgical in how you use social media: I have friends and acquaintances who work in advertising and PR firms. They use social media like a surgeon does. They open it up, go in with a purpose, do what they need to

do and then close it and get out. They don't get trapped inside, using social media for the purposes of entertainment. It's not entertainment, in their view. If you adopt this mindset, you will find yourself being more purposeful in how you use social media. You might want to set a timer, say for 15 minutes, and when it goes off, pull yourself out of social media. I use a social-media planner, where I sit down once every three months, and schedule all of my posts – these tend to be quotes from books, writing tips, productivity tips, video advice, and so on. In between, I will only add posts when I might be at an event, or someone has posted about one of my books and I need to respond.

- Read books and listen to podcasts: As an author, I would recommend reading, but there is something to be said for taking things in slowly and allowing the brain to process them. In his book *The Shallows* (2010), Nicholas Carr makes the argument that the brain is like plastic, and any regular activity changes it.[12] So high usage of the internet changes the brain. It alters the brain from a "linear, literary mind" to one more used to skipping over the surface of information as "skimming is becoming our dominant mode of reading". He says we're losing our ability to concentrate, even to read books. Whether you agree or not with Carr's hypothesis, the point of bringing it up here is that when you are deep in the weeds of reading a book, you have your literary mind engaged and you shouldn't switch it into skimming mode; otherwise, you will be left short-changed by your ability to think deeply. The same can, to some extent, be said of podcasts, which involve a slower, more thoughtful conversation as opposed to a live radio debate. This slowness provides us time to think and ponder on what is being said.

- Walk with purpose: If you live close to nature and greenery, try to take walks there. If not, then just go for a walk wherever you live. To be truly with your own thoughts, on occasion, don't listen to anything – no music, no podcasts, nothing. This will allow your brain to do the heavy lifting in the background, making the connections between ideas, which, when you are constantly receiving stimuli, you aren't able to process. Other times, think about all the things you are grateful for – the beating of your heart, the fact that you have food and shelter, the sky and the stars above. Sometimes, at the start of the walk, mull over a professional problem you might be trying to solve, then push it out of your mind and enjoy the pleasure of walking. You may find you have a solution to the problem by the time your walk has ended. Or at the very least, you have the presence of mind to know how to tackle the problem. This is particularly the case with more emotive problems. What I've learned from taking regular walks is that initially the hardest thing is actually making the time to take the walk. However, if you can learn to schedule walks into your timetable every day, you will soon start to see the benefits, professionally and personally. As with all other suggestions,

start small and build up the minutes. On the weekend, take the family or friends out on longer nature walks.
- Write by hand: One study published in the journal *Frontiers in Psychology* found that regions of the brain linked with learning were more active when participants in the study completed a task by hand instead of on a keyboard.[13] The researchers also found that writing by hand could promote "deep encoding" in a way that typing does not. Another study compared students who took notes by hand with those who directly typed up notes into their laptops.[14] They found that the students who used laptops wrote down word for word what the professor said, whilst those who wrote by hand were more likely to listen to what was being said, analysing it for important content and "processing information and reframing it in their own words". When the students were asked conceptual questions about the lecture, those who had taken handwritten notes were better able to answer than those who had typed their notes. I always take notes by hand during meetings and interviews, and before the end of the day, or at the end of the week, type these up, so that I've catalogued them and can share my notes with others. You can apply writing by hand to professional activities, but you can also apply this if you would like to keep a diary where you can write down a stream of consciousness – the important aspect of keeping a daily diary is that you set a specific time every day and

then stick to writing during that period. Remember, you are only writing for yourself, and the very act of writing will help you remove other distractions and find more purpose in your own life. Writing a letter to your future self is also an interesting way to make the transformation from where you are today to where you want to be in the future. Write the letter, seal it, set a date for when you will open it, set a reminder, and then forget about it for the next couple of years.

12.5 Key points

Some of the critical points we covered in this chapter were as follows:

- When we immerse ourselves in a craft and leave the digital world, it makes us more human, and we obtain a deeper satisfaction from the activity.
- Performing a craft improves well-being, and if you can add a social dimension to it, studies show that this brings additional therapeutic benefits.
- Take up a craft or use your leisure time in a manner that is more in line with your purpose in life. Some things to try are: repair or construct something with your hands, or sign-up to a social or community activity.
- Renovate your life, and decide what you will do in your spare time. When you fill the void with meaningful

pursuits, you will find the digital distractions you used to be consumed by suddenly appear trivial and frivolous and will melt away from your horizon.
- When we set boundaries, there will be some opportunities we miss, but if we don't set them, we can become spread too thin and will be distracted, which does not help us fulfil our purpose and meaning in life.
- Human qualities, such as intellectual skills, can be cultivated as long as you have a growth mindset.
- To defy the attention merchants, ask yourself what the social media or equivalent platform actually does for you that is meaningful. If you need to use platforms like Facebook, consider how it brings value to your purpose in life and then limit your use to that only.
- Resist the attention merchants by doing the following: make social media invisible on your smartphone, be surgical in how you use social media, read books and listen to podcasts, walk with purpose, and write by hand.

Endnotes

1. Gary Rogowski, *Handmade*, 2017.
2. Jill Riley, Betsan Corkhill and Clare Morris, "The Benefits of Knitting for Personal and Social Wellbeing in Adulthood: Findings from an International Survey", *The British Journal of Occupational Therapy*, 15 Feb 2013.
3. Minna Huotilainen, Mimmu Rankanen, Camilla Groth, Pirita Seitamaa-Hakkarainen and Maarit Mäkelä, "*Why our brains love arts and crafts*", February 2018.
4. David Sax, *The Revenge of Analog: Real Things and Why They Matter*, 2016.
5. S. Nicholson, *A conceptual model of the library gaming experience. Everyone Plays at the Library: Creating Great Gaming Experiences for All Ages*, Medford, NJ, Information Today, 2010, pp. 23-30.
6. Wilhelm Hoffman et al., "Everyday Temptation: An Experience Sampling on How People Control Their Desires", *PsycEXTRA Dataset 102*, no. 6, 2012.
7. Brian Resnick, "The Myth of Self-Control", *Vox*, 24 November 2014.
8. Carol Dweck, *Mindset*, 2006.
9. B. S. Bloom (ed.), *Developing Talent in Young People*, New York, Ballantine Books, 1985.
10. Tim Wu, *The Attention Merchants: The Epic Scramble to Get Inside Our Heads*, 2016.
11. Jaron Lanier, *Who Owns the Future*, 2014.
12. Nicholas Carr, *The Shallows*, 2010.

13 Audrey L. H. van der Meer* and F. R. (Ruud) van der Weel, "Only Three Fingers Write, but the Whole Brain Works†: A High-Density EEG Study Showing Advantages of Drawing Over Typing for Learning", *Frontiers in Psychology*, 8: 706, 2017.

14 Pam A. Mueller, and Daniel M. Oppenheimer, "The Pen Is Mightier Than the Keyboard: Advantages of Longhand Over Laptop Note Taking", *Psychological Science*, 23 April 2014.

Chapter 13
EPILOGUE

What I hope *Distracting Ourselves to Death* has conveyed is the importance of living a life of meaning and purpose. This starts by first removing distraction from our lives so that we bring attention to what is necessary and ignoring what is not. When we cast our gaze back on the life we have lived, at work, at home, what do we want to see? A list of tasks we completed or something more meaningful, a legacy that we have left behind for others.

Much of this will hinge on how you use your time. How you free yourself up from always being busy. Make the effort to understand what you value most in life and how technology can assist you with what you value, not become the source of value itself.

Try to live a full life, where you take pleasure in the journey, for the enjoyment and learning come from the steps along the passage of life itself. Reflect on the rhythm of the journey and don't stress about where the voyage will take you. You will end up in precisely the place you are meant to be. Wherever that is, make the best of the situation. What you must try to avoid doing, is chase after the destination, the goal, the outcome, as you will reach a point in your life when you ask, "Is this it? Is this what life is all about, the next thing to tick off my to-do list?"

You innately know there is a lot more to life than just chasing goals, but you will only discover how true this is by removing distraction from your life, so that you can journey inward to discover your purpose, and then journey outward to be in the world.

Along the journey, if you take time to reflect, you will meet others, perhaps in a worse-off situation than you. Take a moment to stop, to help, for this is where you will find the true source of happiness and contentment. Remember, it's your story. It's for you to decide how you live it, to identify what really matters, to be at peace with the choices you make. So choose well.

Chapter 14
ACKNOWLEDGEMENTS

Every book contains the personal cosmology of the writer, how they see the world, and the beliefs and values they hold dear. *Distracting Ourselves to Death* is no exception.

Yet the coalescing of a personal cosmology cannot happen in a vacuum, and so there are a number of people I must thank who have helped shape my professional experience and, in some way, have compelled me to write the book that I have written.

I must begin with one of my oldest and dearest friends, Irfan Mahmood, without who I would not have learned the art of being persistent and fighting one's corner. Barry Smith, for telling me very early in my career that I was his "tip for the top" – that meant a lot. Richard Spencer, for giving me my first big break in a corporate setting, and trusting my ability when there were those who doubted I would succeed in the role he hired me for. David West, for taking me on board for a role which, at the time, seemed out of this world, and which kick-started my extensive opportunity to travel over the coming decades to many parts of the world. Ann Wood, for being a fellow team member and great supporter till this day. Andy Hill, for shielding me into a role when so much seemed to be changing around us – we were in a new millennium, the dot.com bubble had burst and we were searching around for a direction.

My first international posting was as a result of a quite circuitous route, in which I ended up in a role I had not intended to do, but was clearly destined for me. For this, deep thanks go to George Middleton for connecting me with the right people. To Ian Dench, for taking me on a business transformation and handing me a list of 100 tasks on my first day, with the title at the top – *Mission Impossible*. It definitely proved to be in many regards and I must also thank Peter Kaliaropoulos for allowing me the opportunity to continue the journey that I started with Ian.

Ehsan Kooheji, for being the embodiment of a technical genius within the mind of an artist – quite the combination. Sunil Baby, for trusting me to teach his students, and Amanda Peters and Agnieszka Kuzniarski, for expanding my teaching brief and initiating my interest to become an educator. Graeme Lowther, for taking me on for a role neither of us was quite sure would be for long and for teaching me the art of analytical thinking. Rupert Wright, for guiding me through the tricky terrain of writing a weekly business column for a national newspaper. Wael El Kabbany, for being a tireless supporter of everything I have done professionally. Seb Hills, for enabling me to embrace my outside academic

ACKNOWLEDGEMENTS

interests and bring them into the office. Nathan Kulinitsch, for continuing where Seb left off and showing me how tasty chocolate koala bear sweets really are. Wouter Belmans, for providing me the intellectual and creative space to bring outside-in thinking into the role and encouraging my artistic pursuits. Piers Schreiber, for sharpening my cognitive frames through our regular chats. Yusuf Jha, for helping me to connect many of the hitherto unseen dots around the topic of distraction and meaning.

There are also a number of members of my family who I must thank, including my wife, Faiza, for being the first sounding board for any idea, good or bad. My children, Yusuf and Imaan, for supporting me, despite hearing about the same topic incessantly. My uncle, Nauman Khan, for his intellectual curiosity and demonstrating what an octogenarian with a sharp mind can do.

Most of all, I would like to thank you, the reader, for spending the hours you have with this book and hope and pray that both you and I can remind ourselves each and every day to do what is necessary and steer clear of those frivolous distractions, for as the title of this book declares, let us stop distracting ourselves to death and instead do something more meaningful.

Chapter 15
ABOUT THE AUTHOR AND RESOURCES

Rehan Khan is a thought-leader and educator who has worked across telecoms, technology, real estate, private equity and executive education. His expertise includes consulting, strategy, innovation, digitisation, customer experience, marketing, and product management.

A trained social scientist, Rehan holds an MA in Applied Social and Market research, as well as an MBA in Strategy. He was a visiting professor at HULT International Business School (2013–16).

Between 2009 and 2010, Rehan was a business columnist for *The National* newspaper and is currently a feature writer for *Gulf Business*.

He is a published novelist. His books include the Carnegie nominated *A Tudor Turk* (2019) and *A King's Armour* (2020).

To find out more about Rehan, please visit: www.rehankhan.com

DISTRACTING OURSELVES TO DEATH

If you would like further resources, please visit: www.rehankhan.com/resources

You can also follow Rehan on:

f **y** **O** @rehankhanauthor

in www.linkedin.com/in/khanrehan

www.ingramcontent.com/pod-product-compliance
Lightning Source LLC
Chambersburg PA
CBHW021435080526
44588CB00009B/538